A Journey *from* Within

A Journey
from Within

Ways to Understand the Self

Dr. Ram P. Ramcharran

iUniverse, Inc.
Bloomington

A Journey from Within
Ways to Understand the Self

iUniverse books may be ordered through booksellers or by contacting:

iUniverse
1663 Liberty Drive
Bloomington, IN 47403
www.iuniverse.com
1-800-Authors (1-800-288-4677)

ISBN: 978-1-4620-2515-2 (sc)
ISBN: 978-1-4620-2517-6 (hc)
ISBN: 978-1-4620-2516-9 (e)

Printed in the United States of America

iUniverse rev. date: 07/11/2011

To the loving memory of my dad

As the Light Approaches

As the new day breaks, light comes into the heart and soul
Accept this light,
Let your emotions lead you down the path,
The path of happiness, comfort, and joy
Extend your hands to the light,
Grab it, and embrace it
Let it touch your every being.

Dr. Ram

Contents

Acknowledgements ix

Foreword xi

Introduction xiii

Chapter 1   Background of the Author 1

Chapter 2   What Forms Your Belief System? 7

Chapter 3   What You Believe Is More Important Than Just
Believing 13

Chapter 4   Elements that Lead to Self-discovery and Awareness . . . 15

Chapter 5   Understanding Your Personality and Knowing
Your Behaviors 25

Chapter 6   Subcategories of Personalities 33

Chapter 7   Discover and Understand Your Awareness 35

Chapter 8   Defining Fears 38

Chapter 9   Why Do You Avoid Fear? 47

Chapter 10   Why Do You Refuse to Accept Things You
Cannot Control? 50

Chapter 11   What Is the Self? 52

Chapter 12   The Truth about the Self 54

Chapter 13   Questions That Help You Discover the Self 60

Chapter 14   Tools to Learn to Help Identify the Self 64

Chapter 15   Goal Setting 69

Chapter 16   Where Are You Now? Where Do You Want to Go
or End Up? 71

Chapter 17   Systems, Processes, and Structure 77

Chapter 18   Family Responsibilities 80

Chapter 19   Reflections 85

Chapter 20   Hierarchy of Life 87

Chapter 21   Steps to Help You Discover and Understand the Self . . . 91

Chapter 22   Steps to Help You Make Improvement to the Self 95

Epilogue 99

Acknowledgements

I would like to thank my family for the tremendous contributions they have made to this book, although they may not know it. My wife, Sadhana, has created an environment for me to be productive and successful with my writings, and she has tolerated my crazy schedule. My mom has always been supportive of all my projects and efforts and has been my biggest fan. I thank my brother, Bruce, who continues to support me in my endeavors. Finally, I thank my mentor and friend, Dr. Shelton Wood, for believing in me and sharing his wisdom and knowledge over the past ten years.

I would like to express my sincere gratitude to Mr. Tarun Puri, who been like a brother to me. Tarun has worked hard in assembling my Web site and the graphic work for this project to make it successful.

I am very grateful to the many people who have spoken with me and shared their personal stories so I can I share them with my readers.

Dr. Ram

Foreword

I am honored and delighted to write the forward to this book for Dr. Ram P. Ramcharran.

As you read this book and consider the facts for an existence beyond imagination, you may well experience a complete about-face in your sense of values and attitudes. When I met him a few years ago, I knew that that someday hundreds of thousands of people would love his book.

He wrote this book, keeping in view the facts in human life that cause endless experiences in pain or bring unexpected joy filled with desire or hope for happiness. However, in truth, that desire or hope never comes as happiness.

This book is not about a question of belief or disbelief. It is a question of honesty and finding the true you. It is about how to recognize your full potential. I leave the ultimate answer to these facts to God, and to the time when I feel we all have to come face to face with the ultimate reality of life. However, in the meantime, this book gives some insights on how to really discover the real you.

What I want to convey to you, dear reader, is the need to consider your existence in a new light—the light of total glory. Once you have understood and integrated this knowledge in the true facets of life, you will have no further doubts about the system or that it works well.

To summarize, the book is inspiring to read, beautiful to experience, and educational on several levels. It is a case study in how to create and present yourself when circumstances go beyond your control, and all you have is yourself.

My earlier reading of his book, *Reflections of Life*, presented all the possibilities that life brings and repeated visits kept me motivated to re-think his exceptional thinking.

I hope you will be as pleased as I am, as you turn the page, meet Dr. Ram himself, and share in his tales of magical wonder.

Tarun Puri

Introduction

Growing up in a traditional and religious Indian Hindu family in New York City, one of the first things I was taught was that I should learn to understand and respect other people's feelings, especially my elders. However, the harder I tried, the more difficult it became to move forward and to understand others. As I grew older, I was supposed to understand life, my surroundings, and self. However, that did not happen as I expected. I experienced too many setbacks and interruptions in my life.

This book will serve as a journey into recognizing what the Self is; what it has to offer you; and most importantly, recognizing your own inner purpose and inner journey. I will demonstrate to you that the Self is not just understanding what you want in life, or what you are suppose to be or do, but how you can be viewed from the outside in and inside out. When people are around you, they are in tune with your purpose. This will show you how to understand the spirituality of your inner journey and recognize that the Self is not just about the ego, but your entire being and essence. The Self is not just the way you think or feel, but the fullest understanding of life and what part you play in it.

Sincerely,
Dr. Ram

Chapter One

Background of the Author

The Change That Made Me the Person I Am Today

Be the change you want to see
—Mohandas K. Gandhi

It was 6:00 p.m. in the evening on September 13, 2000. I was driving to the hospital after executing the most difficult thing up to that point in my short, and for the most part, happy spiritual life. I was returning from a 62-mile one-way journey after filing divorce papers against my former spouse.

I felt homeless and without any possessions because of the messy break up. I had been thrown out of my own house after working hard for many years to earn it. In a matter of a few moments, it was taken away from me. Until that moment, I thought I had been experiencing the worst days of my life. I felt empty, hopeless, useless, depressed, anxious, worthless, afraid, and powerless.

After filing my divorce documents, I drove to see my beloved father who was in the hospital for the fifth time that year. Dad was very ill. He had been fighting a severe virus for over 3 months. He had undergone two open-heart surgeries in ten years and a couple of other procedures to clean up his arteries. This was not a good thing at all. However, even with all those medical problems, his outlook on life was truly zestful—always!

I had spoken with Dad at the hospital the previous evening. He had said to me, "Son not to worry. You will get through the pain you are feeling and you will get past this situation in your life." He said, "This too shall pass, son." These were his ever-familiar words that I believed sincerely because no matter what, he always made me feel better about difficult situations. He always had a way with words that made people feel secure, special, loved, and appreciated. He assured me that life would always be okay.

On my way back to see him, I was traveling with his sister, my Aunt Savie, who was visiting from Canada. She was with me to offer some emotional support during my time of stress and difficulty. I was leaning on her and venting my frustrations about my divorce proceedings and this highly emotional time in my life. I did not believe anything could get worse, but it did.

As I was driving to the hospital, I missed the exit even though I had driven the route to and from the hospital hundreds of times. I had to alter my plan to visit earlier in the day. I had told dad that after finishing at the courthouse I would visit. He had said, "Don't worry. Finish what you have to do and then come see me later in the evening." He said this while trying to smile despite his pain.

With his support and guidance, I was able to make it through a difficult decision in my life. I had decided to do what I felt would be best for my life and get out of a destructive and failing marriage. He had said, "Do what you need to do and the rest will fall into place." This was a very difficult decision to make, especially with the social stigma associated with divorce in our community.

I missed the exit to the hospital because of the rush hour traffic congestion. I was not able to make a U-turn, so I decided to take another way that turned into a traffic nightmare. What should have been a ten-minute delay became a forty-five-minute detour. During the time in my car, I was joking and chatting with my Aunt Savie. We were reminiscing about our family vacation from the previous year when the entire family had visited Guyana, where I was born. It was my first trip back in over twenty-five years. We were talking about Dad's relationship with his own father. Things had been different when he was a young man. At this stage of life, our relationship was better than his had been with my grandfather, which made me feel great at that particular moment.

When we got to the hospital, Savie and I were still laughing and joking as we got off the elevator on Dad's floor. As I was passing by, I could feel all eyes on me. At first, I thought people were staring at us because we were laughing so much and making too much noise. As I went past the nursing station, I noticed the closed door to Dad's room. This was unusual because he never closed the door to his room. I pushed the door open. I saw my mom crying hysterically and noticed that my cousin was holding her trying to calm her down.

My worst fear hit me square in my face. My father had passed before I got there. It was just two months before his fifty-second birthday. My hero and best friend was gone. At that moment, I could see my life was never going to be the same ever again. I felt fear, pain, uncertainty, hopelessness, and anger. The thought that it was a dream and not happening, crossed my mind in a split second.

I was facing my lifelong fear—death! I always avoided death and funerals, but now there was no place for me to run. I felt trapped! The one person in my life that told me how he always felt whether it was good, bad, or indifferent was not going to be there anymore to be my best friend and father. The thought of being fatherless was agonizing and extremely painful.

I heard my heart beating faster and faster. The blood in my veins was racing and the room started spinning. I could not focus. Suddenly I realized I was standing over my father's lifeless body, slapping his face and shaking him vigorously. I was telling him to wake up. I screamed, "You can't leave me, us, your family, your wife, and grandkids." I was living my worst fear and nothing could have ever prepared me for all of the emotions that were taking place. I was standing in a cold hospital room with my mother crying uncontrollably and my life changed forever. I was powerless and experiencing my worst and deepest fear. Losing my dad was the most painful experience I have ever had to live through, but it was also the most life changing and inspirational experience I have ever had. Not a day goes by that I do not think about my dad. His passing and the experiences he shared with me before his death have helped me become the person I am today. He gave me the biggest gift: how to discover the Self. His death set the stage for me to start the journey. I want to share my experience with you because it was the turning point in my life. His passing was the catalyst that helped me understand my fear. It gave me awareness, and most importantly, it has made me understand the Self and put me in touch with my consciousness and inner being.

I will never forget the pain I felt while I had to deal with my father's passing and my own family breaking up simultaneously. It was as if everything around me was falling apart and I could do nothing to stop the pain. I was heartbroken! I was torn up inside! I knew that my life changed, but was it for the best or the worst. I would have to take control of my fears, emotions, mental state, and my Self to define who I would ultimately become. I needed to stand up. I needed to be strong for my family, my son. I had to take charge and control of my being for the rest of my life. I needed to turn my fears into power, take action, and take charge of my life.

Identifying my total being and making the decision to learn who I really am was not a difficult decision. I was forced to make it. If I had not, I would probably be like all the other divorced people who end up bitter and continue to blame the other party for their crappy marriage and difficult, empty, and unhappy state. The realization of where I was and where I wanted to be was miles apart. I always thought I had a good life. I had some loyal friends, a great career, a good work environment, a nice boss, a nice house, and I drove a nice luxury vehicle, but it all fell apart and I felt helpless. Even when situations were supposed to be happy, they were not joyous. Aside from the birth of my son, everything in my marriage seemed pointless and hopeless. When everything came to a boiling point, I felt as if I had no choice. I made a life-changing decision that has given me a life of peace, understanding, love, compassion, and the understanding of my Self. I now know me. The discovery of this state of being is refreshing, joyous, and peaceful. This was the beginning of my inner journey.

Life Changing Experiences

A man of character funds a special attractiveness in difficulty; since it is only by coming to grips with difficulty that he can realize his potentialities
—Charles De Gaulle

One afternoon, I walked in from working out at the gym, when my ten-year-old step son, Rohan, unexpectedly asked me a question that triggered a deep thought and a hidden memory. It was about a life changing experience that had guided my path of life for fourteen years of my young adult life.

I had lived my life in a subconscious bliss, unaware of why I had the academic drive I did, while I was an adolescent, and as a young adult. You may be wondering what caused me to structure my life the way I have. I had forgotten about that experience until Rohan asked me, "Did you ever get left back while you were in elementary school?" I had to think about that question for a moment because I had shared the same grade with my younger sister all through my elementary school and high school years. My friends and teachers used to think my sister and I were twins. I use to say, "No, no, no!" I would ask angrily, "Do we look like twins?"

The truth was that my parents moved us to the United States from Guyana, South America when I was seven years old and my when sister was six. I was placed in the third grade and my sister in the second grade. After about two weeks, my third grade teacher, Mrs. Goldstein, called my parents and said I had a reading problem. She said that it would be best if they moved me to the second grade. In actuality, I was an extremely shy and passive child, who was afraid to read in front of my peers. This made it very difficult for me to function in front of others. I did not like to talk period. I remember thinking to myself that I would have to sit next to my sister all the time: at home, at school, on the playground, and do homework together and that would be too much for me. I was very shy and was I afraid to express myself. What I remember most from this experience, even at the age of eight, was that I was never going to fail at anything academically again in my life. That experience laid the foundation for my academic achievements today.

I remember my sister being far superior to me in all aspects of school. She never had to study as much as I did. She was a very gifted student, while I struggled just to keep up. I had to study and work twice as hard to get the same grades, but I always had the thought in the back of my mind that I was older and just as smart, so I was supposed to be better than her. Unfortunately, that did not always happen, but I was able to hold my own throughout high school. My sister and I were members of the Academic National Honor Society, but her grade point average seemed to always be better than my own. Upon graduation we both won several academic scholarships, I went on to Florida State University, a state school, and my sister headed off to the University of Miami, a private and respected academic institution.

I remember thinking of all the years I had to work so hard because I never wanted to be left behind academically. I had forced myself to work hard and to get ahead academically while my sister coasted. The experience of being put back a grade left a lasting impression in my life that helped me achieve higher education. I became aware of my Self and inner being very early in my life and I did not waste the academic opportunity. This experience is more than likely responsible for my thirst for knowledge and competition, when it comes to achieving, to this day. I am very aggressive in any learning because I honestly feel you can never know too much and that you owe it to yourself to learn and continually improve your life, especially if it makes you more aware.

The real test for me was when my sister and I went to separate schools. My parents used to say, "Vedo is not going to be there to push you any more." I am happy to say that I went on to earn an MBA and a doctorate; and my lovely sister earned her BA in Management and Accounting, got married, and became a wife and a mother of two beautiful girls. In the end, we both succeeded in our own right. I think my parents did a great job in raising us.

Chapter Two

What Forms Your Belief System?

It is our attitude at the beginning of a difficult undertaking, which, more than anything else, will determine it successful outcome.
—William James

As you grow up in the early stages of life, you encounter and experience certain events and situations in your life that program your belief system. Growing up, I was fortunate to be surrounded by loving parents and family members who openly showed their affection. Hugs and kisses were never lacking in my household. I was placed in what most would call a protective and safe environment, but I was allowed to be myself and make my own mistakes.

Aside from the ten years that I lived in New York City, most of my experiences growing up were in extremely safe surroundings, which helped groom my behavior and attitude. Although I lived in New York for just ten years, it shaped the foundation for my independence. I was forced to be a self-starter and an independent child while I lived in the city. I had to take two city buses on my own to get to my magnet junior high school. There was no dropping off or picking up at the car circle like my friends had in Florida. I had to take a couple different trains to get from Queens to the Bronx to help my dad in his drugstore sometimes after school and during the summer because we were expected to work in the family business. These experiences helped me become self-sufficient while I was growing up.

Our earlier life experiences are paramount to forming beliefs and molding who we are. Our belief systems are formed by our values, which ultimately will lead our lives, and determine how we act, function, react, and behave. The belief system encompasses all these areas.

Values: Once you understand how values work, you will be able to understand the true purpose of your belief system. Values determine how you respond to all experiences in your life. When your perceived values are satisfied, you feel fulfilled, rewarded, and happy. When values are violated or unmet, you feel empty, burdened, and dissatisfied. When you do not have clear values, you experience conflicts and stress, and make us feel uncomfortable with the Self and you do not gain realization. When you do not have a clear understanding of these parts, it leads to fear. Values for everyone are different and carry different levels of importance. Some may value their families as their number one priority. For others it may be making money and what it could mean to their lives. Overall, most individuals possess values that are righteous and good natured.

Family Background: Your family background and upbringing play a very important part in forming your belief system. Some of your beliefs come from your immediate family like your grandparents, parents, and siblings are passed on to you through traditions and customs. Your parents shared stories about life when they were growing up or your grandparents shared their experiences, which indirectly helped you grow, and you formed your own beliefs. Without ever realizing what is happening, your beliefs are formed between ages six and thirteen.

Motivation: This is perhaps one of the most overlooked traits in the development of the belief system. Motivation is the ability to put your ideas into action without having to be pushed or prodded by others. The importance of being a self-starter is very crucial to understanding the Self, and making and taking steps towards the realization of your being. Not everyone shares the same level of motivation. Once you figure out what your purpose is it will lead to action, which leads to understanding of your being and what is important to you.

Environment: Your surroundings affect your development and your beliefs. For example, a child that is raised in the lap of luxury is more likely not to have the same outlook on life as a child who was raised in the projects of Harlem, New York. The surroundings one is exposed to at a very early age make a significant contribution to the long-term views and beliefs held throughout life. However, your environment is just one factor in determining who you really are. Today, we find many people using their environment as an excuse for their lack of respect, lack of success, lack of manners, lack of responsibility, bad decisions, and poor judgment.

Ethnicity/Heritage: Your heritage and cultural traditions will determine some of your beliefs. Each race and nationality has a certain way of doing things and has beliefs and traditions that they carry from generation to generation. Indians, Italians, and Jews as well as other nationalities have traits and beliefs in their people, which are cultural in nature and make up their beliefs systems. Obviously, they will all have different ways of looking at life. Their beliefs are not bad, just different and there is nothing wrong with that. We must just learn to recognize and accept others for who they are.

Fear: Fear develops because of many things that transpire in our early childhood. Many of us never realize where we get our fears. The onset of fear can cause you to become paralyzed in your daily life. Your fears control and restrict your beliefs. When we experience fear, we tend to limit our growth, potential, success and realizations could be. This in turn limits the Self, its development and growth. Fear is one of the key elements in how you think, react, and believe. If fear leads your life, you truly cannot experience anything positive because you are never focused or aware of what is happening around you. You are limited in your development and you settle for less in life. Find ways to conquer your fears!

Your attitude and being are established between ages eight to thirteen. Your belief system starts to form and eventually you choose the path that will guide you for the rest of your life. Unless you experience a life-changing event or situation, you will always have your beliefs. However, when all this is happening, you really do not know your subconscious is governing you for the most part. So be aware of how you handle certain situations.

Every so often, a situation occurs that will forever change your life, your belief system, your thoughts, and thinking process. It is as if someone turned on the light in your consciousness and you discover the Self. It is realization of your life's purpose all at the same time. BAM! It hits you like a ton of bricks. You become fully engaged. The problem with this is that you have to actively choose to take action on self-realization or it will evaporate just as if it never came. For the most part, many people never choose to make the decision to pursue their Self discovery and their new-found realization because they would rather keep the status quo. They forever wonder why their lives are the way they are without attempting to understand it. Many never follow through on trying to find themselves because of one or more of these reasons:

- You do not understand or recognize what is happening.
- You are afraid and fearful of change.
- You wait too long, the subconscious takes over, and all is gone until the next life-changing experience occurs. It is my suspicion that these experiences only come once or twice in a lifetime, so if you do not act or take action to investigate further, it is lost and most likely gone forever.
- You accept and settle for the same old everyday life cycle.
- You have a lack of belief; faith, spirituality, and no focus, motivation or drive.
- You resist because it means giving up something. This is the easy way of dealing with their everyday life.

Let me clarify a few things. I previously mentioned about the Self, which I believe starts to evolve between ages six to thirteen, or at least by the beginning of adolescence. During this time of growing up, what you would most likely turn out to be in turns of attitude, behavior, values, and motivation is determined. I firmly believe when I was at that age, I knew what my beliefs and values were. However, I did not know what I was feeling nor did I understand what these thoughts were. What I am trying to explain is that while going through these experiences and making choices and decisions throughout your growing years, at times you do not act on events and situations; you just react because you are already predisposed and your raw instincts take over. During those early and formative years, you ultimately shape your life for the better or worse, but you change and make improvements and different choices once you recognize what is happening.

We learn early on to accept our fears and live with them. It starts to limit self-growth, development, outlook, values, goals, motivation, responsibilities, and your personal self-awareness. You have to recognize every day that your life is a new day for self-discovery, self-awareness, and personal growth and you must harvest that development each day. You must address your fears and face the things that you fear. You gain awareness and then you can understand the Self. I will expand in detail about the makeup of the Self later and its importance. However, for now I will offer just a glimpse of what to expect.

Educating the Self, understanding and managing fear is a lot of work in the early stages of a person's life because it means accepting changes. Facing your fears, setting new expectations, forming new goals, creating visions, reassessing your values, and keeping your motivation will mean learning to associate with others with similar or entirely different beliefs and outlooks on life, which will help you gain a better pulse of your surroundings. After learning all that, would you be ready to make a change or would you be afraid, fearful, and apprehensive of making the decision to change? Because they are afraid to accept and make changes to improve their life, many people stay in the contemplation stage indefinitely. When you contemplate, you constantly think about an event or situation without taking any action on your thought or desires.

First, let us look at the things you need to understand so you can face your own fears and learn to discover the Self. I will provide you with some tools and give actual examples. They will help you understand how to discover, evaluate, and correctly identify these situations so that you can move towards self-awareness and start to understand the Self and find realization and inner discovery. This could mean the discovery of a new world.

Chapter Three

What You Believe Is More Important Than Just Believing

Happiness can't be found when we are yearning for desires. Make a note to yourself to start thinking more about what you have than what you want. Treasure yourself.
—Dr. Richard Carlson

In order for you to make a difference in your life and to know who you are, you have to establish and identify beliefs and core values. What you believe is more important than just believing. Just believing you will be rich is okay, but believing in hard work, dedication, and commitment to a purpose will make you rich and successful. This thought process has direction. You can use those tools to become rich but believing with no action serves no purpose. It is the first step towards understanding who you really are. Many people fail and succeed each day. What is the difference between one over the other? Both at one time believed they were going to be successful in their business, but one differentiated success and failure. It shows how and what you believe is what makes the result different. Your beliefs have to be realistic. Let's face it: no matter what I believe or do, I will never be able to dunk a basketball. I am five feet, four inches tall. I can believe all I want that someday I will be able to dunk a basketball, but it will never happen, especially if the basketball rim is ten feet high. When you have beliefs, you are taking a stance for something. When you take a position and make a commitment and then when actions are applied, you move towards self-awareness.

Chapter Four

Elements that Lead to Self-discovery
and Awareness

They are able because they think they are able.
—Vergil

Freedom

With understanding the Self, there is a natural process that every person has to battle within himself or herself repeatedly. This is how you find the thoughts of freedom. What is it and how do you achieve it? I think what happens here is that you start to realize that freedom itself has to do with your inner Self. If you can think and act independently, then you are free from ties and emotional bonds.

When you have too many issues that you have to deal with constantly, this does not allow you to act the way you want. Right or wrong, there is a process to employ to get things done and moving forward in your life. For example, if one continuously rebels against someone or something, that really means that someone or something has control over the other. Sometimes rebellion is confused with the sense of seeking freedom. What they see is, "I am getting my way," and that is not freedom at all. Freedom is your capacity to take a hand in your own development. I believe true freedom is man's removal from bondage and emotional struggles. Once you get to a certain level of consciousness then you are free to act and do what you believe and think is correct for yourself.

The accomplishment of man's freedom goes back to his past and upbringing. I do not believe everyone is given the same tools to succeed. The more love and devotion you receive as a young child, the quicker you achieve freedom. This will happen only if you are given responsibilities early in your youth and you are held accountable for your actions. Once you have attachments tied to bondage and carry hang-ups and unresolved issues, you will never achieve inner freedom. Freedom and self-thinking go hand in hand. Freedom only comes when you are ready to accept things that you cannot control and you proceed with life as if it is your first day of life on this earth!

Conscience

It may be all right to be content with what you have; never with what you are.
—B.C. Forbes

The difference between man and animal is that man can make active choices, and animals cannot. Humans can make a conscious decision and that is what differentiates us from animals. Human beings not only can make choices of values, morality, ethics, and goals, but he must do so if he is to attain integration with other men. Man is the ethical animal, but he does not just grow into an ethical being. He is molded by his surroundings and teachings, his desire. His ethical uplifting comes from him battling with his consciousness, ethical awareness, inner conflicts, personal inhibitions, fear, and anxiety. Once you experience these emotions, then you can becomes conscious of your total being. Until then, you are lost, wearily seeking to find the Self.

Dr. Rollo May said, "Those who take a rigid view either of religious or scientific truth become more dogmatic and lose the capacity to wonder; those who acquire the wisdom of their fathers without surrendering their own freedom find that wondering adds to their zest and their conviction of the meaning in life." I believe his statement sums it all up; because it allows us to take the wisdom of our elders, loved ones, and respected peers and still have the capacity to retain our own thinking and natural ideas which give us the ability to explore and deduct for ourselves. You have to remember no actions are entirely pure and that you, as man, must learn to accept all actions and have certain levels of motivations in order to achieve and find the Self. Your decision to do the right thing is what makes you special. Conscience for everyone is different but universally when it's for the betterment and for the good of man, it's always favorable.

Courage

Never, never, never, never, never give up!
—Sir Winston Churchill

Courage is your ability to be yourself while always being open to new ideas and being willing to experience new things. You have to experience many different stages of life as you grow from a child, youngster, and teenager all the way to adult life. Discovering your courage will help you find the Self and help you gain awareness. It will lead to full engagement. Courage is an extremely important part of your character and makeup as a person. Courage is used to overcome your feelings of insecurity, anxiety, and neurotic behavior, but the tough part is recognizing the need to improve your life. Usually, people lack courage because they are afraid of being abandoned and being isolated from their family, friends, peers, or colleagues and the things they like.

Courage is seeing and accepting the truth and being able to live with your life's failures and successes. This is the beginning of discovering your growth, allowing change, and having awareness of the self. The courage to recognize and act on these feelings will bring awareness to your inner being and will define you and your character. Courage is not being a "tough guy," but the ability to recognize, make, and take action to self-improve and discover what is within you. Courage drives your freedom, your character, your dreams, goals, and the discovery of the Self.

Patience

Make the most out of the best and the least out of the worst.
—Robert Louis Steven

"Good things come to those who wait." I believe that statement is essential to understanding the Self. You see, we live in what I call the self-service and fast-food society. If you drive through any major city, you will find a super Wal-Mart on an average of every five miles, as well as a large chain of self-service gas stations attached to a modern-day fast-food restaurant and convenience store. We have become a society of quick and easy. You are finding less family-owned eateries and more national chains that are capable of pumping out a meal and fake atmosphere, which fulfills the quick and easy need. People expect things to happen right away and during this process, they miss the important things in life. We seem to be always rushing to get from point A to point B. When you have patience, you also have a tendency to raise your expectations for better results. When you are quick and unfocused, you settle for less and expect to give up far more for the same results. The phrase, "patience is a virtue", did not just appear overnight.

Getting answers to a question immediately is not always better and completing an assigned project the next day does not guarantee success. Patience is truly an important component of the Self you need to embrace. When you are able to find and discover this simple trait and use it appropriately, you will find a new world of awareness. Learn it! Accept it! Count on it! It will take you to the next level of your inner being. I guarantee it.

Your Self

The more extensive a man's knowledge of what has been done, the greater will be his power of knowing what to do.
—Benjamin Disraeli

They are many different thoughts when it comes to identifying the root of discovering the Self. The loss of values in this era, and how things differ today than from the renaissance period, is a key factor in understanding the Self. The loss of the sense of Self and dignity of human beings is directly tied to the breakdown of human consciousness and awareness. One of the continuous themes throughout human concern is the loss of the sense of the significance and the worth of the Self. To understand the Self is to understand the loss of personal communication. I strongly believe that along with the loss of the sense of the Self, society has also lost our language of communication with each other. If this feeling is one sided, it will lead you to loneliness. The lack of personal communication and effective language is making it impossible for us to communicate correctly and effectively with our fellow man. Have you experienced this yourself? If you have, how do you solve it and how do you prevent it from continually happening?

We need to improve our relationship with our Self and nature because nature does not go away; it eventually takes over its surroundings. We can change by moving from our surroundings. You need to learn to improve your life by eliminating emptiness and handling your anxieties because when you make life situations a problem, it is difficult to experience the wonders of your surroundings. The drowning out of the senses is a tragedy and it is important because you need to understand that life and humanity have significance. You must have respect for human life and all it represents.

Dr. Rollo May wrote, "We could go farther and point out that finding the center of strength within ourselves is in the long run, the best contribution we can make to our fellow men. This is what our society needs—not new ideas and inventions, important as these are and not geniuses and supermen, but persons who can be, that is, person who have a center of strength within themselves." You need to make this world a better place for yourself and your fellow man.

Becoming a Person

The secret of success is to do the common things uncommonly well.
—John Rockefeller Jr.

Consciousness of the Self is the distinctive characteristic of each man. Each man determines his own mark based on his actions. We now understand that whatever you do is a reflection of your past, your upbringing, and your experiences as a young child. Some of you experienced a wonderful childhood and that eventually leads to higher consciousness and success. As you start to understand the Self, you will be able to determine your own behavior and identity. One way to understand this process is to reflect on your experiences and this will help lead you to understand your behavior and consciousness. As man grows, his understanding for others will mature as he experiences new events, which will lead him to develop his own character and thoughts. This brings you closer to knowing the Self.

Self-Contempt

I have often regretted my speech, never my silence.
—Publilius Syrus

Many people do not handle this area very well. Some believe it is okay not to be confident. That it is a cover up for your lack of self-worth. Understanding higher consciousness is to understand you first. When you understand your own Self, then you can offer others advice that will have an effect. Selfishness and self-love are opposites and when you understand the differences and act on them accordingly, it will bring you closer to understanding yourself.

The more self-awareness a person has, the more alive he or she is, and then more consciousness will be attained. Becoming a complete person means a heightened sense of awareness and experiences. The "I" mentality is removed and a sense of others takes precedent in your thinking. Look beyond the obvious and explore. You deserve consciousness. Get ready for a wonderful ride into knowing yourself and discover what the possibilities can be.

The Struggle to Be You

Nearly all men can stand adversity, but if you want to test a man's character give him power
—Abraham Lincoln

The process of becoming your own person is tied directly to your parents, especially your mother and how that development was established, and how that relationship is expanded and replaced. The main struggle relates to you moving out of the protective love that your mother showered on you while growing up and moving away from that dependency to new independence.

The struggle is learning how to deal with that anxiety and the feelings of being powerless when you are on your own. The struggle that you feel is internal. When you handle or learn how to deal with that emotion, then the sense of consciousness arrives and allows you to understand and act appropriately. When you experience the realization of being independent then you are truly on your own. Experience it! Accept it! Live with it! There is no better feeling of being self-sufficient in this world. It is one of the most rewarding feelings in the world.

Understanding

Every man takes the limits of his own field of vision for the limits of the world.
—Arthur Schopenhauer

Let us talk about being considerate to others. It helps you become more aware and it leads to the discovery of the Self. Let us look at this event: a man was on a plane and he was reading his newspaper when a father and his three young children got on the plane and his children started making noise. The man reading the newspaper started fussing and asked the father to calm his children down and he told his kids to be quiet. The children stayed quiet for a little while, but started acting up again. The man trying to read the paper started to get perturbed again so he said to the father, "Can't you control those brats?" The father turned to the man reading the paper and calmly said, "I just can't get myself to yell at them because their mother just died this morning and I don't think they understand what has happened." The man felt awful and quickly changed his attitude towards the children and started to be friendly and wanted to comfort them with kind words. You see, sometimes you need to be understanding and tolerable because it allows you to become more aware and in tune with the Self. You will never know when you will need to be comforted.

Expectations

A wise man will make more opportunities than he finds.
—Sir Francis Bacon

You see, expectation is vastly important when it comes to understanding the Self. Setting expectations is an essential part to knowing the Self. When you know what your expectations are, then there is no disappointment, just fulfillment. What happens most of the time is that you set yourself up for failure because you have unrealistic views and expectations in your life and of others around you. What you need to do is raise your own levels of expectation in order to become more aware and productive, but at the same time setting guidelines and rules about how you plan to reach those expectations. If you have no directions and you expect to do something that is impossible, you will fail to achieve it. You are certain to be disappointed, leading you to feel bad or upset. Set your expectations, but be realistic in nature and once you are able to do so you are on your way to discovering the Self. The correct expectations are paramount to gaining awareness and realizations. Expectations are crucial to gain growth. You must be able to accept your successes as well as your failures. You must accept the results of the expectations you set and eliminate any faulty thinking you may have. If you are able to do so, you are again closer to realization and understanding the Self.

Attitude

It is our attitude at the being of a difficult undertaking which, more than anything else, will determine it successful outcome.
—William James

In the words of Lowell Peacock, "Attitude is the first quality that marks the successful man." If he is a positive thinker, who likes challenges and difficult situations, then he has his achieved success. On the other hand, if he is a negative thinker who is narrow-minded and refuses to accept new ideas and has a defeatist attitude, he hasn't got a chance. You see, attitude is everything when is comes to beliefs and getting ahead.

The Self is discovered sooner when you are able to recognize that your attitude has a lot to do with the results you are getting. When you encounter a tough situation, your attitude will ultimately be responsible for the outcome. You see, at times your attitude can be more important than a fact because your attitude will be your guide in how you seek to handle a difficult situation. Your ability to maintain a good attitude during tough times will play a strategic part in gaining awareness and discovery.

I am fortunate to be friends with a man who has a great attitude. His zest for life and success is extremely contagious. His ability to find the positive in the negative is very enlightening. Tim Burkhardt, has been a tremendous inspiration to me. Despite experiencing some personal difficulties and situations in his life, Tim has maintained a great attitude through it all. At one time, Tim found himself, at thirty-eight years old, incapacitated from a severe back injury. This left him financially unstable with a family to support because he was out of work for over a year and half. However, his positive attitude towards life getting better never wavered.

His attitude was that he was going to get through the difficult time he was experiencing. His attitude to succeed carried him during the hard times. It brought him closer to gaining self-awareness and self-discovery. Tim said to me, "Ram, I was so low that there was no where other than up for me to go." He experienced feelings of hopelessness, uncertainty and despair but he truly believed that he would succeed at something. He did not know what it was going to be at the time, but he believed his positive outlook and attitude would carry him through the rough times.

One day Tim was introduced to a business opportunity by an old friend at a company called AMS Marketing. After learning about it, he quickly believed that he could make this a career where he was going to help people and at the same time provide a living for himself and his family. The requirements for this opportunity were talking and a positive attitude. Tim possessed both of these. His attitude guided him through because he felt he could now make a difference to his family and the people around him. He felt the products introduced to him could help make a difference in people's lives. Not only did Tim do well at talking, believing, and having a winning attitude, he has become one of AMS Marketing's top producers and supporters. He achieved platinum level, the highest position one could reach in the company, in just six months. Today, he continues to improve his life each day. His attitude and belief towards his business has helped him steer many people in his network marketing business. He has shown hundreds of people how to realize their dreams by sharing his ideas, beliefs, and a positive winning attitude.

Chapter Five

Understanding Your Personality and Knowing Your Behaviors

Every man has four characters that which he exhibits, that which he has, and that which he thinks he has and he believe.
—Alphonse Karr

To understand who you are, you must learn to understand others and how they think, react, and speak. This way you can accept who they are. When you are able to identify others' personalities and behavior, you are in a better position to interact with them.

There are four main categories of personalities to learn to understand how you act and think. I will discuss and focus on four subcategory personalities and behaviors that are associated with these personalities and work in conjunction with combinations of actions. Together, they will help you better understand yourself and others around you.

The Advocating Personality

In my opinion, advocating is the first personality and behavior you need to know and understand to learn about self-discovery. This style of thought is consistent with distinct traits that include tendencies like creativity, with an intuitive nature. This personality will look at the bigger picture or the overall environment, when making a decision or commitment. A person with this type of personality usually looks for unique solutions much differently from the norm. This type of personality is usually dynamic in thinking and extremely colorful, animated and excitable, enthusiastic in conversation, and responsive to questions.

This person needs to be involved in the decision-making process. They want to be stimulated as they view the big picture. Their need for recognition, attention, and visibility must be satisfied before you can influence change, commitment, or decision from them. In order to initiate changes, or a response for a decision, you must be very creative in your approach or your efforts will be ignored or be considered boring. When exploring the decision, you must make your approach with expression, feelings, emotion, and excitement. This personality will not allow change to take place without having you display extreme efforts. When offering solutions, you must have a unique and well thought out plan in order to create interest and emotion. Keep in mind when developing solutions you must strongly consider their contributions, ego, and thoughts about the solutions, which stress concepts; not necessarily all the details are required to be described, but you must display an overall vision and impression to the approach. Some of the objections that hamper decision or commitment may sound like, "This same old approach, is there a better idea, did you consider my idea." These few objections are typical of what their behavior would display. Once you understand what the thoughts are, it is a lot easier to formulate an approach to understand said personality and behavior when it comes to decision-making and commitment.

Let us look at Jim, with his advocating personality. How will he be able to understand himself? He needs to feel as if he is always in control and in order for him to look inside his being, he will need to feel as if he is making the discovery for himself to continue to see and understand the Self. Are you this personality? Who do you know that is this way? Read on and discover you. Understanding others personalities can and will help you discover the Self.

The Friendly Personality

The next major category of personality and behavior is the friendly individual or personality. This characteristic is distinctly different from the previous behaviors and personality described in the last paragraph. This personality type is more people-oriented, warm, and expressive in their approach to things and to life in general. They are very animated and like to be called upon for help because they are naturally supportive people, who display a great deal of patience and understanding during certain situations and crises. This personality type is very accepting of others. They are very easy to talk with and do not necessarily probe beyond the conversation at hand.

You can probably have an influence on them easily because they are not focused on the larger issues or problems outside the discussion or current. They like to engage in small talk and appear very content with life. They are very trusting of others, usually to the point where others sometimes take advantage of them.

The friendly personality and behavior's needs are unique from the other groups. This person needs to have acceptance and needs to feel a sense of friendship and bond. They like to know the directions of others and like to show concern. Before making decisions, they like to gain approval and acceptance so they feel liked by everyone. This group will avoid confrontations and will take the path of the least resistance. They are very adverse to risk. This personality group's emphasis is on responsibilities to others rather than to themselves. They will not take risks when it comes to them vs. others. They have a high regard for others and themselves. They are easygoing and do not like to be pushed or made to feel pressured, and they like to be perceived well by others.

The person who possesses this personality usually will have objections that sound like, "It's different." They do not particularly like change or deviation from routine. Consistency is important to their surroundings. This group likes to put things off, especially decisions. They say things like, "I would like to think about it," or "I would like to discuss it with others." They are very positive people so they give you a false sense of approval, but they are extremely non-committal in their decision-making process. This person is very aware of what others think or may say. When they cannot make decisions statements like, "My people won't like it," may surface.

How does understanding personalities help you learn about the self? Think silently for a moment. My friend Mickey likes to feel as if he can help anyone and everyone because he is always looking for acceptance from his peers. Sometimes, he does this to the extent that he neglects his own needs. Do know anyone like this? Do you fit this description?

The Analyzing Personality

This personality is very difficult to understand, but once you learn this personality you will know a lot more about people. The analyzing personality is another major behavior and personality, whose group has many distinct characteristics and modes of action. This behavioral category has tendencies that are also unique to the personality. This person tends to be extremely disciplined and well organized to the point of being overly dogmatic in their thinking. They like to be low-key and tend to stay away from groups or crowds. They do not like to be the center of the conversation or the party, and tend to feel more comfortable in small groups or in a one-on-one situation. The perception of this personality is that they are very competent and unimaginative in their thinking. They like to walk the straight line. Everything must be done by the book. The precise approach is how they execute and perceive things should go.

With this personality, the other party is normally carrying the conversation because they are too busy thinking and not necessarily paying attention to what is happening around them. Their behavior is reserved and very controlled. They usually support the status quo and choose not to rock the boat when it comes to changes or making influences on some issues. This person is viewed as being technically sound and superb in their task, profession, career, or job. What excites this person is usually what they are working on. They become so engrossed in what they are doing that it seems at times the world is at a standstill. This persons needs are very simple and few.

Their behavior calls for security. This personality needs to feel comfortable and needs reassurance that they are correct when thinking and making commitments and decisions. This is how they feel and gain acceptance. This personality likes technical challenges that are extremely logical, and they pay particularly close attention to details associated with projects and tasks. What is extremely important is that they like to feel that they have knowledge in whatever they are attempting to conquer or master.

The emphasis for this person, in general, is quite difficult to figure out and understand. This behavior and personality likes to deal with logic and lots of structure. This means when attempting to gain commitment and approval, you must be very thorough and stay away from risky situations. When attempting to get an answer or decision, they will more than likely want to explore situations and answers already proven, ones that are not difficult to explain or figure out. They like to take the easy way of solving or accomplishing the task. They have no need in reinventing the wheel. When attempting to explain, one must demonstrate and prove the usefulness of the project, service, product, or situation being discussed. One must display a technical superiority in order to gain approval or commitment from this personality type. Once a decision is made, it is well thought out and firm.

The most common obstacle when trying to understand or deal with this personality type is the constant requests for supportive evidence. You must constantly show proof in order to gain approval or commitment in whatever you are attempting to do. This personality is looking for you to demonstrate your technical skill in order to achieve closure on a topic. This person may show interest, but will always be reluctant to act right away unless evidence or proof is provided in the very beginning. They do not like to have to figure anything out. They do not like difficulty, the smaller the gray area, the better the result. Frequent objections would be, "This is too complicated," and "It will be disruptive the current patterns of what I am doing or trying to accomplish." Sometimes to break the preoccupation with a situation, they will say, "I would like to think it over." However, they will play the scenario in their mind repeatedly. Making a decision is very difficult for them because they are saying, "I am too busy to consider it," or "When I am not as busy, I will get around to it."

This personality and behavioral pattern is extremely difficult to gain commitment from unless one displays and applies all the counter traits described. You are probably wondering how is this going to help you understand the Self. Remember, you are trying to discover your personality. Is this your personality or do you know someone that possesses these traits? Bob, my neighbor, has this type of personality. He is a computer programmer and constantly wants me to prove my entrepreneurial ideas to him before I can gain his support. He is constantly reviewing the data to make sure everything adds up.

The Driven Personality

The next major personality and behavior is the driven personality and behavior. This personality type also possesses some unique traits that are very different from the other personalities described earlier. This person tends to be the take charge and controlling style. They display a sense of formality and protocol in their behavior and decision-making process. They are more focused on the situation, service, and product, and are not particularly interested in people. They are extremely direct, sometimes to the extent being rude or arrogant. They are usually forceful and aggressive in their approach. They do not want to think it over or consider this or that. They normally would hide their desire or emotions with a stoic approach.

When trying to understand this person, remember their thoughts are not to be sucked into or tricked into anything. They are always looking for something better or cheaper. They imply competitor's offers of cheaper rates are better when discussing business, sales, or a decision. This person is extremely critical and is naturally distrusting of other people in general. They come across as being busy and they have no time to waste. They are always on the go, and very impatient when dealing with other people. They will always challenge the status quo. One must constantly prove himself or herself in order to gain commitment or approval. They are usually quick to make decisions and it is difficult to change once a commitment is made. This personality displays know-it-all behaviors. Their tendency is to overplay or overstate expertise or knowledge. This person avoids chitchat and small talk because they believe there is no time to waste in the day. Time is money! The day is short enough already! Do not waste time.

This personality and behavior group's needs are not lengthy, but they are extremely difficult to please because they have the win-win attitude and behavior. They are constantly looking for instant results and actions. You only succeed in their eyes by displaying your achievements. Life is a big bull's-eye. They are looking to hit their targets at all costs and they want results not excuses. They are extremely impatient. One extremely important need and concern is to be in charge. They must be allowed to lead. When looking to explain this group, we must look at the emphasis, which is a strong focus on saving time and money. They want value at all cost. The perception is that they are cheap.

A unique behavior is their increased need for control over others when in a position of leadership. This personality and behavior is constantly looking for compliments and wanting achievements. This is how they seem to find their happiness. There must be a constant stroking of their ego. They want to be known as the leader, not the follower. However, this group does not have good followers, but they are perceived as being good leaders. This group is extremely difficult to please because of their emotional and behavioral makeup. They are short tempered and want you to get to the point. You must focus on the objectives at hand, with no deviation from the point discussed. If it takes too much time and money, it must be too difficult to complete or achieve. Their objections are, "How can we measure your results when looking to have this done or accomplished." They are very difficult to please because they are constantly looking for something better. They have a tendency to think the competition may be better, so they ask, "What good are you doing for me?" They see no reason to change unless they see value. They do not want to be associated with things that will waste time and money and are results-driven. This personality is very difficult to deal with. However, once you earn their trust they are extremely loyal.

After reviewing the main differences of all the characteristics of these personalities, you should be able to understand which personality fits you. If you are not clear exactly where you fit, you will find some other tools to help you discover the Self and personality. One of my former colleagues was a driven person. He expected everyone to come to work early, stay late, and do exactly what he said. He served as a company commander in the Army and felt everyone should be the same way he was.

Chapter Six

Subcategories of Personalities

Men acquire a particular quality by constantly acting in a particular way.
—Aristotle

Assertive, reserved, outgoing, and *flexible* are the four subcategories of personalities that are important to understanding personalities and behaviors when it comes to understanding the decision process. Learning and understanding these sub traits will help you recognize people quicker. These four subcategories are important. They will help in understanding what personality and behavioral patterns will come about and how they relate to the decision process in your life. When you look at these other behaviors or personalities, they are not the leading factors when we describe or identify personalities. However, they are the ones that help explain and assist you in understanding personality patterns and tendencies

The four personalities described will encompass at least one of the four groups. When you look at the friendly personality, you will more than likely find that person is also very flexible. A flexible personality is willing to compromise, share ideas, and is open to new thoughts and suggestions. When you associate with a flexible personality, you will find that person also possesses some analytical traits as well. A flexible personality will show these two tendencies and traits.

The next combo of personalities likely to go hand-in-hand is the reserved persona. This personality is very quiet and shy and is not very outgoing or talkative. They are intimidated by others and require prodding in order to move forward with decisions or with the opposite sex. A reserved personality may possess some analyzing behavior traits. The reserved type is not going to be your hard charging person. They are the intellectual types who are not risk takers and are willing to stay and go along with the status quo. The reserved personality is not your leader type but your academic and follower.

The next personality subcategories associated with behavioral patterns are the assertive and outgoing subgroups. When you examine personality and behavior more closely, you will find the assertive and outgoing person to be more influential when it comes to the association with the driven persona and the advocating persona. These combinations are very likely one way or the other. You will not particularly find reserved driving persona but will find assertive and advocating with some driven traits. These combinations allow you to understand behavior and personality better because it is difficult for one personality to dictate and function by itself and to lead behavior.

The next subcategory is the outgoing personality. This group is very helpful to understanding the friendly and advocating type traits. When you find an outgoing person, they are usually very friendly as well and willing to help. They are looking at the big picture. The outgoing personality is unique because you will find advocating people who also posses friendly traits and behavior as well. The key to this whole exercise is to give some examples of what personality you may be yourself which will help you gain understanding of the Self. By providing you with this information, you will have useful and identifiable action steps you can use to gain awareness, find your inner being, and learn to understand others. If you are able to understand and connect the points on how to identify these traits and characteristics, it helps you identify who you really are and when you can do so, you closer to knowing the Self.

Chapter Seven

Discover and Understand Your Awareness

Man lives by more affirmation than by bread.
—Victor Hugo

For you to know the Self, you must become more aware of what is happening in your life. Are you going through the motions of getting up and going to work, coming home and cracking open a six pack of beer, watching the boob tube and going to sleep after watching the 11 p.m. news to start the same routine over again in the morning? Well, if that is your routine, do not feel too bad because you are not alone or much different from the rest of the people in our society today. We have become the most unaware group of people in a half of a century. We are in a society of quick fixes that are fast and convenient. Whatever happened to being in tune and aware of people and your surroundings?

Steve, an acquaintance of mine, is a prime example of someone who is unaware of what is happening around him. He would miss meetings and key elements of conversation at work, and then he would wonder why his business was not growing and his promotions and earnings power stagnated. Steve sabotages his success in two ways. First, he does things incorrectly because he does not listen, so when it comes to following simple directions he is lost. Secondly, he avoids doing things that he does not like doing at all costs.

When you are not aware mentally, you cut off your feelings and emotions with others, leaving you open to make mistakes. In the case with Steve, all he had to do was make a decision to become more aware and listen carefully. He could have facilitated this by improving his thought process simply by writing things down right when they were presented to him.

To further your growth and discover your awareness, you must have a clear understanding of what you want to change in your life. You must work on heightening and growing your inner and outer awareness. There are three levels of awareness you must learn and understand:

1. *Being aware of something after you've done it.* Jon, a smart, handsome, and dashing young doctor, had a tendency of going overboard with giving his new girlfriends gifts and luxury items in the beginning of their relationships. However, after a while his efforts of giving the gifts wore off on the girl's because in reality the gifts were a replacement of his time and commitment. Being a doctor his schedule is very unpredictable so he is not always able to keep his dates and engagements with his girlfriends, so he would send expensive gifts because he felt bad. After his fourth lost relationship in one year, he quickly realized and became aware that he has already experienced this pattern before and that he was not going to do it again.

2. *Being aware of something while you are doing it.* I am sure you have experienced this feeling. Think back on occasion you were not going to eat sweets for a whole month or consume a particular food, but you found yourself eating that chocolate bar, or a slice of pizza or guzzling down that cold sweet tasting can of cola. I had promised myself I was not going to consume any more than 300 grams of carbohydrates in a day. One day, I was so hungry that when I was in the mall I went to the food court intending to order a chicken Caesar salad, but instead I ordered a double cheese slice of pizza, which happens to be my favorite food. As I was taking my second bite, I realized what I had done. I became aware of something I was not supposed to do while I was actively doing it.

3. *Being aware of something before you do it.* This is when you are in tune with your consciousness. This is very important in the stages of change. When you can recognize this and become aware, it is remarkable because it takes a while to break the cycle of being unaware. If you find yourself going to do something that you know is either good or bad for you, this will help you identify that you are going to be better off.

The question to you as a person is what will determine your ability to continue to be aware? Effort from you, time, and patience will teach you to become and stay aware. Once you realize, you will less likely repeat the same mistakes you made. Discovering and understanding your awareness will make you a better person. It brings you closer to self-discovery and helps you take aim at learning who you are.

Chapter Eight

Defining Fears

The man who does things makes many mistakes, but he never makes the biggest mistakes of all—doing nothing.
—Benjamin Franklin

Fear is defined as anything that prevents you from moving forward, taking action, or making a firm decision within your life. If you have not been successful in handling fear, you have not identified your true fear(s) yet. What you have to do is find out what your real fears are. Identifying your true fears will open your entire being to the reality of your surroundings and to your inner person. This will bring you closer to self-awareness and understanding the Self.

Anxiety and apprehension do not prevent growth they can help stimulate it. Alternately, fear paralyzes and prevents exploration, vision, and the establishments of dreams and goals. You have to find a way out of these self-imposed torments and inner prisons. Learn to make fear a tool for progress and growth, not handcuffs as if you are a prisoner. Identifying your fears and retooling your thoughts for use as a mechanism for growth and progress. Turn your fears into action and power! Act on it! Make it serve you.

When you cannot escape fear, learn to tame it, understand it, and embrace it as a way of enhancing progress. Only you can transform it into a companion that accompanies you in all your exciting adventures. It is not an anchor holding us fixed in one spot, but a stabilizer for progress and growth. When people have told me repeatedly that they are never afraid it leads me to question them almost immediately. When I question them more in detail or ask specific questions, their responses are always lacking substance and usually it boils down to semantics. Yes, they have and experience fear! Yes, they feel nervous, anxious, and apprehensive, they just do not label it as fear.

As we move forward in life, it is possible that some people do not feel or experience fear, and they become so in tune with the Self that fear is an afterthought in their daily existence. I am certain of one thing: I have not met anyone without fear thus far. Deep down inside, we all have a fear of something. We must honestly admit it and then we choose to deal with it. The surface of our consciousness is okay. The subconscious needs convincing and redirecting to think differently, and you must learn to accept and redirect it so that you can discover the true Self.

I have learned to feel fear and accept it for what it is. It happens to be a tool for progress, personal growth, realization, and self-awareness. Always remember that when you feel fear, first you must accept that it is there and then you must act on it, appreciate it, and redirect it into positive action. This will help bring about changes and new awareness. Your life will always be okay regardless of the level of fear. You just need to recognize it. The main difference is the guilt you feel at times when you know fear is there and you do nothing to get a grasp on it. The mere existence of it affects you.

Truth about Fear

A. The fear that we feel will go away as long as you continue to grow and develop your life and Self.
B. The only way to get rid of your fear of something is to go out, face it head on, and do what makes you fearful. Tackle it directly. Conquer it! Most of all identify it, and accept it for what it truly is and turn it into power and action. Do not let it control you or your actions!

C. The only way to feel better about the Self is to go out and do what the self is really telling you to do! One major problem is that if you do not learn to recognize those thoughts and feelings, you will never know what could be. Listen to your inner Self.

D. Remember, not only are you going to experience fear whenever you are on or in an unfamiliar territory, place, or situation, but so is everyone else. You are not the only one who feels this emotion. Others have the same similar fear. I am okay. You are okay. The Self can accept and understand experiences and feelings. Count on it!

E. Pushing through your fear is far less frightening than living with it. Fear is the result of feelings of helplessness. Once you face your own fears—you must accept it and reflect on the results or consequences, and then you can make adjustments and make redirection. Turn it into a tool, not a hindrance in your life!

Types of Fears

According to your own experiences, the level and intensity you feel when fear occurs will be determined by your inner being. No one can ever tell you your fear level is silly or stupid because no one experiences the same level of agitation you are feeling. What you may see as being extremely fearful may be a passing event for another. For example, for many years I was deathly afraid of heights. Going up stairs, riding in an elevator, or crossing a bridge was a horrible experience for me, but for many it may not be a big deal at all. Telling me that looking down and seeing open space was a not something to fear a few years ago would have made us enemies, but today climbing ladders, going up stairs and crossing bridges is just another passing event for me. I faced my fear and conquered it by understanding and identifying it. I became aware and accepting of things I cannot change or control. I finally understood the space between the height and me would not change regardless of what I felt. I learned to accept it and I am better for it today.

Fear has many different faces and levels and many people suffer from all sorts of fears: falling, failure, success, death, aging, moving, the list is endless. Whatever you can possibly think of, someone out there is afraid of it!

Fear can be categorized into three levels:

1. Surface fear
2. Inner state of mind
3. I can't handle it

I believe there is another level of fear that should be identified. It is the ego level. The ego has a lot to do when it comes to how you change, make decisions, think, and respond to your life issues and circumstances you cannot control. The ego has a tendency to dictate your life without you ever knowing what is happening.

Level One: Surface Fear

Let's examine surface fear, which is broken down into two categories:

Category A: Fears of things that just happen

*   Aging
*   Becoming disabled
*   Retirement
*   Being alone
*   Grown children leaving home
*   Natural disaster
*   Loss of financial freedom
*   Change and evolution
*   Dying
*   Illness
*   Getting robbed
*   War
*   Time passing
*   Gravity

- Loss of physical movement
- Losing a loved one
- Accidents
- Rape

The types of fear that just happen are things you normally would just take for granted. Some are harassing and disturbing but you have a tendency not to question what happens in everyday life because you expect these things to happen.

Category B: Fears of things that require action

- Going back to school
- Making decisions
- Changing career, position, job
- Making new friends
- Ending or beginning a new relationship
- Using the phone
- Asserting oneself
- Losing weight
- Being interviewed
- Driving
- Educating the self
- Pollution
- Starting a new business venture
- Spending time with a loved one
- Moving to a new location
- Public speaking
- Making a mental error or mistake
- Intimacy

Take a moment and review the lists above. What are your thoughts? How many of these fears have you experienced? If you experienced them, how did you handle it? Fear does not discriminate. It touches every part of people's lives, sometimes unconsciously, but many people struggle with fear and understand it cognitively. For example, fear can affect the simplest things in life. Things we take for granted, like making new friends. If you fear meeting new people or being in unfamiliar places, then going to work at a new job, going to parties, or socializing becomes a chore, or tiring and an extremely difficult thing in your life. It would immobilize you, causing you to feel miserable and stressed.

Level Two: The Inner State of Mind

The inner state of your mind is the subconscious. This is very closely related to the ego yet very different. You should know by now the subconscious is an accumulation of events that took place over time and will ultimately show up in your outlook, behavior, and personality. It determines how you react during certain events and situations. This state of mind is crucial since it is not "situation oriented." It involves your subconscious. Here are some examples of level two fears:

- Rejection
- Success
- Failure
- Being vulnerable
- Being conned
- Helplessness
- Disapproval
- Loss of image

All of the events are not situations or actions. They are reflections on your sense of the Self and your inner and outer ability to handle everyday life. The states that I have listed thus far are all reflections in nature. Let us look at disapproval as an example. If you are afraid of disappointing your parents, friends, or peers, this fear will affect almost every phase of your being and your day-to-day existence will be painful. Approval, or the feeling of acceptance, is extremely important to everyone's life. This is especially important for personal growth. Learning who we are and what we are is thoroughly important to understanding the Self.

Rejection is a horrible feeling to accept and to deal with. It is very similar to disapproval since it plays an intricate part in personal development and growth. Rejection is rejection, no matter how you look at it. No matter where it is found or experienced, it is still rejection. Whenever you experience fear, or what you perceive as fear, you automatically begin to go into a protective mode to shield the Self, which is your ego. Consequently, you completely limit your personal growth. You close the world out and shut down your consciousness. You cannot move forward or see beyond the fear at hand because fear possesses you and paralyzes your being.

Level Three: "I Can't Handle It"

Level three's fear is very powerful. It is the biggest fear of all. This type of fear is the one that really keeps you stuck in your old non-functioning and non-progressive state. During your day, you may be consumed by feelings of "I can't handle it!" Those feelings may be overpowered by feeling of "I give up!" At the bottom of every one of your fears is simply the fear that you cannot handle whatever life has dealt you. When you experience this level of fear, it is important to recognize that you still have options in your life. It is crucial to keep a positive outlook and an upbeat attitude.

Let's Review

Level 1 fears

- I cannot handle making a mistake.
- I cannot handle illness.
- I cannot handle losing my job.
- I cannot handle getting old.
- I cannot be alone.
- I cannot handle making a fool of myself.
- I cannot handle not getting a job.
- I cannot handle not losing him or her.
- I cannot handle losing my money.

Level 2 fears

- I cannot handle the responsibilities of success.
- I cannot handle failure.
- I can not handle being rejected

Level 3 fears

- "I can't handle it period."
- "If you knew you could handle anything that comes your way, what would possibly have to fear?" Nothing!
- "I am giving up!"

With level three fears, you have to eliminate your fears and understand the Self. The way you do so is to develop more trust, patience, and understanding in your ability to handle whatever comes across your path. This goes back to your ability to believe and perceive. This takes courage and action. If you are determined and willing to work towards it, you will find yourself. You just have to look. "Seek and you shall find."

How Do We Conquer Fear?

Let us look at some affirmations that will help in reducing and eliminating fears. You can use these affirmations to help train your thoughts to work through your fears.

- I can overcome in the face of adversity
- I have the courage to change
- I have the courage to feel and face my fears
- I can take risks and succeed
- I can turn obstacles into stepping stones
- I have faith which helps raise me above my fears
- Why worry?
- I choose not to have fear.
- I choose courage, faith, peace, and love over my fear.
- I turn fear into enthusiasm, excitement, and anticipation

As strange as it may sound, or how corny it may seem; this process of affirmations works because it is telling your brain that you are in control, not your emotions. Try it. You will discover that it really works.

Chapter Nine

———

Why Do You Avoid Fear?

Fear of failure: We hide it. We deny it. We fear it. We ignore it, and we hate it.
—Anonymous

Your fears can come in many forms and patterns. Simple things become stressful and irritating. Most of the time you avoid making decisions or situations that make you feel uncomfortable. Avoidance is the short-term solution to a long-term, embedded, deep-rooted problem or fear. We all avoid fearful situations to feel a sense of being in control. When you retain control over your behavior and environment, it makes the fear we have to face easier to live and deal with. I will give several detailed examples later to demonstrate why you avoid fears. Avoidance of painful and fearful situations is tough to understand. Your ability to live with these fears and painful emotions is crucial in dealing with and understanding why you fear. Some people refuse to attempt to confront or accept their fears. As soon as the situation that leads to fear occurs, they become so insane that they do not know what they are doing.

Reacting to their fear becomes priority. They refuse to acknowledge the situation or fear. They do everything to avoid this pain. I hinted to this before and I will go further into detail on how to understand the subconscious and its reactions. These people create grief and stress for themselves and initiate ongoing reactions because of the fear and apprehension. What is sad about fear avoidance is that it is transferrable to your spouse, children, family members, and co-workers without you really realizing it is happening. It is important to recognize this situation because if you do not, it will create and perpetuate this cycle over and over, making it difficult to break this mode.

My closest and dearest friend refuses to accept certain things she cannot control or change. Because she does not want her son to worry about anything in his life, she takes on his stress and turns into fear of not knowing what will happen with his life. It turns to fear of letting him grow up, which ultimately leads to her becoming overprotective. I know some of you are thinking, "What's the big deal?" All children at one time or another have to face certain difficulties and situations at in their lives. The realization of being alone and having a child is very important to her. In fact, nothing else in this world and in her life matters more to her. As a parent, you do everything for your children. The fact is, when we feel a certain way, no one has the right nor should say that you should not display a behavior or show an emotion.

I want to draw a picture of this. When the issue of avoiding pain or fears for another consumes your being then it becomes unhealthy. You are not able to be fully effective in dealing with issues or situations that may arise. In this case, Lilly constantly worries that she needs to ensure her son is not feeling pain or anxiety. She feels she must attend to his every want and desire, and when she is not able to handle a certain situation for him, the problem consumes her and puts her in a state of tension, stress, and constant worry. Her son goes to his father's home every other weekend for his scheduled visitation. His dad is not a very nice person to Lilly and constantly manipulates his son by telling him things that upset the child.

This in turn puts Lilly into a state of stress and anxiety, which ultimately turns into fear of rejection and abandonment. Her fear of not being able to see and feel her son and her thinking that her child is not happy while he is away from her brings on negative reactions and feelings of anxiety. Not accepting that she cannot control what happens when the child is not with her, upsets her, and limits her will to be happy. She automatically becomes abrasive, distant, angry, short tempered, and irritated with the people around her.

I would like to think that after three years of having to face the situation that Lilly will be able to recognize and accept her ex-husband's behavior. What needs to happen is that Lilly has to understand it is not her fault or doing and that she needs to let the situation unfold naturally. What happens is that she wants to remove the condition and pains that her son is experiencing. She would much rather transfer the pain onto herself. I believe any good parent, like her, would not want their child to experience pain or difficulties. The two things that are worrisome are not that Joshua's dad is still mistreating her and mentally harassing the child, but rather it is that Lilly still allows herself to get agitated and eventually starts to limit the growth of Joshua by becoming overprotective. This limits the child's experiences, events, and situations based on what she deems comfortable. She feels the child should not be placed in difficult situations that would make him uncomfortable, hurt, or cause him to experience fear.

What is tough to understand is when someone knows what the situation is and knows the cause, but continues to make the same mistakes repeatedly. Accepting less of them is difficult. Especially when they say, "This is the way it is and I will handle it in time." That response says I am not facing fears, and I prefer to avoid confrontations. Avoidance is what it is. Why would anyone want to think that way?

This ultimately comes back to being willing and able to understand the Self, which will bring you closer to realization.

Chapter Ten

Why Do You Refuse to Accept Things You Cannot Control?

We are free up to the point of choice; then the choice controls the chooser.
—Mary Crowley

I have an acquaintance that refuses to accept that he cannot control everything in his life. He has been in a dead-end relationship for over three years and he experiences the same issues and problems continuously, but he refuses to do anything about it. All he does is say, "I know, I know, but I love her." She continues to disrespect him, belittle him, and disregard his feelings, but he still sticks around. Why does he accept less and give more and more of himself? Because he has not accepted his life for what it is, and what part he plays in it. His lack of his self-respect and lack of his self-esteem keeps him in this situation.

What is disappointing is that many people have tried to help and point out the negative relationship that he has been experiencing only to be ignored and criticized for not entertaining his ideas and perception of the situation. That is because when you are so close to a situation you become blinded by the emotions that surround the situation.

Sometimes, you need to stop worrying about things you cannot control and be self-directive and sufficient. Only you will be able to determine what the situation is by digging deep down inside your head and emotions. You must learn to accept things for what they are. That does not mean that you have to like it, but accept it for what it is. Only when you accept can you can move on in your life.

Chapter Eleven

—————

What Is the Self?

All this is full. All that is full.
From fullness, fullness comes.
When fullness is taken from fullness,
Fullness still remains.
—The Isha Upanishad

The Self is one, although it may appear to be many. When you meditate and concentrate on understanding it and begin to realize your mind and body it leads you to self-discovery. Once you see the Self in everyone, then you can appreciate life for what it is and what it brings. Ultimately, the Self is pure and desires only good things. It wills nothing bad and nothing that is wrong. You should seek and realize the Self for your own satisfaction. Those who seek and realize the Self will fulfill all their desires and attain their dreams and goals. Self-discovery shows we all live in this world because you want to desire good. Without this in your life, you will have emptiness, wander aimlessly, carry low self-esteem and have locked up anger.

The Self is your being! Those who realize it, will understand their consciousness, gain awareness, discover realization of your purpose, and enjoy life. When you become aware of your consciousness, love and understanding of the Self will be sustained. You can then stop belaboring things you cannot control and not be tied to things that render you powerless. You must turn fear into power. When we attain those things, we can then take action to make changes. When this happens, you discover that it is better to need less than to have more. As the venerable Mahatma Gandhi once said, "There is enough in the world for everyone's need; there is not enough for everyone's greed."

The Self is understood once you take the time to recognize the power it possesses within you. Learn to accept who you are and you find the Self.

When you start to understand and recognize the above statements as truths, you can recognize the existence of the self as the true ruler of you, instead of controlling behavior, a career, or an addiction. Those who deny the existence of the Self are bound to continue to make the same mistakes repeatedly. Once you recognize this, there is the freedom you seek. Only then, will you understand your own being. The Self is within you and it is up to you to recognize it! Remember, the Self is blind. It is up to you to give it sight. Once sight is attained, all the greatness of you and the world will be found. You don't have to search any longer. The discovery of the Self will keep you occupied because there is so much to learn, experience, and see around you!

Chapter Twelve

The Truth about the Self

Before anyone can become successful in an environment with the unstructured character of the trading environment, one needs to develop a supreme sense of self-confidence and self-trust. I am defining self-confidence as an absence of fear and self-trust: knowing what to do at the moment when it needs to be done, and then doing it without hesitation.
—Mark Douglas

Are you creating your own misery? If so, you can create your own joy and happiness as well! The Self has many definitions, explanations, faces, and descriptions, but the way I want to explain it is very simple. The Self is what you want it to be! There it is. It is that simple. There is nothing more. Once you learn to set realistic expectations, the result is your life will be more in line with the reality of your surroundings. The Self wears many hats, and until you define its role you cannot expect it to function productively. The many facets of the Self are amazing. It has relevance when it comes to

- Spirituality in that it processes your belief in a higher being or purpose
- Inner being and its striking force dealing with your consciousness

- Realism and Expectations by addressing how you set your goals and how you measure the results
- Mind set by addressing how you understand self-realization. This goes back to not being tied to only one way of looking at life.
- Levels of Knowledge because not only are there different levels of education, but there are also different levels of openness when dealing with or handling difficulties.

Cognitive Understanding because it allows you to think beyond the obvious by digging down deeper into your inner being and extracting your most guarded thoughts and fears. The Self is just not a place hidden within you, but the essence of what makes you whom you are. Most importantly, it is what we all live for.

Let us explore various thoughts about the Self. Most people of western understanding and culture do not look at the Self as a form of spirituality, but attach it to a person's being. When I reference the Self and its explanation, I am directly referring to the spirituality of a higher being. I am not targeting or discussing any particular religion or faith because all religions in their own right possess and advocate goodness, spirituality, and inner peace. Usually a version of the Golden Rule is expressed, which refers to treating you neighbor the way you wish to be treated.

Spirituality can be stated as believing in God, the supernatural, a higher power, or the omnipotent in this process. It is recognized through prayers, mediation, and blind faith with the belief that there is a power out there that is higher than man is.

The role the Self plays in this process is one of calming, peace, understanding, patience, pride, growth, flexibility, compassion, acceptance, tolerance, and honesty. Your spirituality will bring us closer to knowing yourself as a person and as a human. You are supposed to gain realization through prayer and meditation. Once you practice those basic rituals, the understanding of the spirituality and prayer will bring you closer to understanding the Self.

Another way to focus on trying to understand the Self is how you refer to the inner being. The inner being is your intuition. This is the natural way of dealing with your fears, excitement, thoughts, and thinking. Most of the time, it is pushed aside because it is not something you have ever developed as a person. The inner being is what I call the intuition. How many times have you had a certain feeling about a situation or event and did not act on it and low and behold, it comes out exactly like you felt it or saw it happening. From speaking to my patients and colleagues, many of them believe there is a way of activating your intuition and your natural ability to feel your way through situations. Remember, the Self has many different facets. It may come to you as a sense of belonging, a sense of comfort, and a sense of feeling accepted, but not necessarily from spirituality although it may bring out discovery and connection to it.

The third part of the Self is realism. Realism is very difficult to explain because you have to address the importance of setting and understanding your own expectations. When you have a realistic outlook, you are not hurt, disappointed, or scrambling for answers, and it gives you a sense of certainty. Then you can really be who you are and that is the path to personal development. The understanding and acceptance of who you really are is crucial. Realistic expectations can come in so many different forms and when they are placed in the right situation, it brings greater pleasure. For example, how many times have you placed your frame of mind in the wrong place by having an unrealistic expectation from the very beginning? For example, say you went to Las Vegas with the expectation of turning $1,000 into a $100,000 and not losing any money along the way. Your sense of realism is skewed from the very beginning. You placed the Self in a situation to lose because the moment you lose you trigger defense mechanisms, which put your thought process in the shut down mode. The Self wants realism. Realistic thoughts, understandings, and expectations are necessary for the Self and inner being to be developed and recognized.

The fourth facet of understanding the Self is your personal mindset. Your mindset refers to your inherited and learned behaviors. They were culturally instilled in you when you were growing up or were gained in the environment that you were placed in or raised in. It is extremely important for you to understand and realize when you are faced with a certain situation or difficulty you naturally respond the way you were taught. Without thinking, you react and handle the situation. For example, I talked about fear and how progress can be paralyzed by fear. Well, it is very similar here as well. It is very common for a parent to teach a child to limit themselves in growth and progress by constantly saying things like, "Be careful today when you are leaving the house." What that statement is saying is that you are not responsible enough to take charge and complete a task. The limiting statements that parents make become ingrained into a child's subconscious and when they are faced with a difficult situation, the inner Self and mindset take over regardless of it being good, bad, or indifferent.

The subconscious is like a tape recorder. It records all the commands you receive and stores them and your thoughts play them back when you least expect it. You really do not know when unless you access all the tapes to ensure you keep all the quality messages and discard the bad ones. The only way you will accomplish that is by learning to understand the Self and recognize what is truly happening around you at all times. You must become fully aware. Please do not confuse concern with faulty thinking here.

The fifth facet of discovering the Self is your level of knowledge. Knowledge has nothing to do with how smart you are or how much education you have attained. Knowledge has to do with how much you know about that particular subject. We all know many individuals, friends, colleagues, and family members who are doctors, lawyers, engineers, and senators who have no knowledge about who they really are. They learn about academics and they fail at understanding and discovering who they are. Take a moment. Think about that and reflect on it.

Education does count a little. I will not totally discount it because hopefully the more educated someone is, the more open they are to exploring their personal growth and learning to understand their inner being, but that is not always the case. Another component that does not apply to development of the Self is your level of wealth or your community status. Here are a few examples of people who had it all: money, fame, glamour, and they never learned how to understand who they really were. They never understood the Self. Elvis Presley comes to mind. I loved him, his music, movies, and his charisma. He had the world at his feet, but he never seemed to be happy. He could not get a handle on his emotions. He never had a grip on his life, his inner being, or his self-worth. He abused his body regularly with drugs and alcohol. He used these vices to abuse his life. He could never understand why he was that way despite being a nice and decent person. He never learned about the Self.

Another rich and famous person who comes to mind because she never found happiness or really understood herself was the beautiful and talented Marilyn Monroe. Not only was she talented and beautiful; she was very self-destructive. Marilyn never understood what happiness and her life was all about. Like Elvis, she also abused drugs and alcohol, which finally led to overdosing on pills taking her young life. Today's world is still no different for the rich and famous, but there is definitely an attempt these days to find out about self-worth, inner being, self-discovery, and understanding the Self as an entity. The sad part is that no matter what your wealth or status is in society, everyone is capable of finding and understanding the Self.

The last facet of the Self can be discovered through cognitive thoughts of understanding. This is the process of thinking beyond the obvious. This is the deepest thought into the inner being and extracting the most hidden feelings. However, this process is an active decision. To learn the Self, you must journey to the cognitive behavior to open your thoughts and understanding. This will lead you to exploring your own inner being and wants. This will help you make a change and understand why you think, act, believe, and do the things you do. I firmly believe it takes a special breed of a person to do so. Usually the cognitive approach to understanding the Self is a proactive way of handling fear. Fear is triggered by a life changing experience or a challenge, which forces you to seek and dig deep down into your inner being for an answer. This ultimately brings you to the discovery of a part of your life you never knew existed. Once you see what unlimited potential has been hidden for so long, you will spend a great deal of time on self-discovery. You must try to understand it to understand its realization and accept the personal growth and self-improvement that it has brought your life. This opportunity should be used to tackle the inner fears you may possess and force these fears into action and move forward to improve your life and Self. This becomes an essential part of living your life freely and uninhibited without worrying about things and situations you cannot control.

Many people think that is why they struggle to handle fear and understand who they really are, but understanding the Self is not that difficult, although it takes effort and desire. I would ask my friend Lilly repeatedly, "Why be miserable when you can be happy and not be affected by things you can't control or definitely change?" If you apply positive thoughts and thinking, which can be a difficult task to do and accept, you will be able to expand your thoughts and enter into a state of realization to understand what is important in your life. According to Dr. Shelton Wood, a psychologist with the Army Institute of Training, It is reported that over 90 percent of what you worry about never happens. That means that our negative worries have about a ten percent chance of occurring. If this is so, then it is possible that being positive is more realistic than being negative. Think about how you are. Think now. Most of what you worry about, stress over, or fear may never happen. Are you being realistic when you worry all the time? Focus on what you can control! Why be miserable when you can choose to be happy? In the case of how Lilly thinks or reacts when she worries about her son is classic fear avoidance. "Nothing is realistic or unrealistic" says Dr. Jim Lin. It is only what you think about and perceive in any given situation. You create your own reality. I know what you are asking, "What does that have to do with fear?" It has everything to do with it. Removing and understanding fear is critical to your self-discovery. Fears keep you immobilized and push you in directions you ordinarily would not go.

Chapter Thirteen

Questions That Help You Discover the Self

Self achievement is no guarantee of self-acceptance.
—Sidney Harris

- What are my goals?
- What is my vision?
- Who am I?
- What makes me who I am?
- What is important to me?
- Who is most important to me?
- Why do I stress?
- What causes me to stress?
- What are my most important values?
- What are my beliefs?
- What is my purpose in life?
- Why am I the way I am?
- What do I do for myself?
- What do I do for my family?
- What is my purpose in life?
- What do I do for my community?
- How do I want to be remembered?

- What do I want to be remembered for?
- Am I successful?
- Do I feel as if I have failed in my life?
- Whom do I love the most?
- Who loves me the most?
- What are the most important things to me in life?
- Who are the most important people in my life?
- What gives me strength?
- What or who gives me inspiration?
- Where did I get my values?
- From whom did I get my values?
- What is my pet peeve?
- What makes me happy?
- Do I feel satisfied with my life?
- What do I need to change in my life? If anything?
- What are my biggest fears?
- How do I handle my fears?
- Do I handle my fears?
- How do I get away from my fears?
- Why do I have fears?
- How do I describe the Self?
- How do I describe who I am?
- How is my relationship with my parents?
- How are my relations with my siblings?
- Am I understanding of others' feelings?
- What makes me excited?
- What are my dreams?
- Am I willing to change?
- Do I see beyond the obvious?
- Am I a good listener?
- How patient am I?
- Am I compassionate?
- What are my priorities in life?
- How do I plan to get where I need to be or go?

- Do I feel as if I belong?
- Am I a leader or follower?
- What would I do differently if I were sixteen again?
- Am I satisfied with my life?
- Am I satisfied with my education level?
- Do I feel that I am knowledgeable about the world and life?
- Do I feel smart?
- What am I most proud of in life?
- Do days feel short or long for you?
- Is my career satisfying?
- Am I searching for life's answer?
- Do I daydream?
- Do I constantly look for new opportunities to improve my life?
- Do I prefer the status quo?
- Am I outgoing?
- Do I prefer peace and quite or prefer noise and distraction?
- Is my life rewarding?
- Why do I worry?
- Do I feel as if I am making a difference to others?
- What worries me the most?
- Do others like me?
- Do others respect me?
- Am I flexible?
- Do I have low or high self-esteem?
- Do I believe in a higher being?
- What is my spirituality?
- Do I believe in faith?
- What is my favorite place in this world?
- What is my favorite color?
- Am I overweight?
- Do I exercise regularly?
- Should I write my eulogy?
- Where and who am I loyal to?
- If I die today, would I be satisfied with my life?

- How many bad habits or vices do I have?
- Do I volunteer or give to charity with regularity?
- How much community service am I involved with?
- What am I doing to improve my well being?
- Do I love myself?
- What do I consider success?
- Where am I in my life? Accumulation, sustaining, retired?
- Am I interested in self-discovery?
- Do I mediate?
- Do I have faith?
- Am I artistic in nature?
- Do I like to travel?
- Am I adventurous?
- Do I place restrictions on my life?
- What are my taboos?
- Where would I like to retire?
- Where would be the one place I would like to visit?
- Am I a needy person?
- Am I giving?
- Am I a self-starter or do I need direction constantly?
- Do I feel happiness in my life?
- Do I feel like I know who I am?
- Do I feel understanding the Self will make my life more rewarding?

Chapter Fourteen

Tools to Learn to Help Identify the Self

The most rewarding things you do in life are often the ones that look like they cannot be done.
—Arnold Palmer

Spirituality

Spirituality is what I call the gateway to the knowing the Self. I am certain at one point in time or another you have asked yourself why are we here in this world? What purpose do I serve on this earth? Are there other life forms out there in space as you stare up at the stars? Are you wondering why you have been placed on this planet? If you have not thought about why you are here then you have not entertained the presence of a higher being. No matter what your faith or your God is, do you believe there is a presence of a higher being? No matter what happens in life, in order for you to discover the Self, you must possess some form of spirituality. Spirituality is part of the sum of the Self.

Spirituality is discovered from the inner being and has different meaning for everyone. It is the perception of the other world and its makeup. Spirituality can be refined through meditation, yoga, prayers, visualization, openness, and consciousness. Spiritually teaches us that the Self does not die nor is it born. It is developed through discovery and awareness. It resides in you. It goes far beyond the senses and the ego. Developing spirituality leads you to awareness, which leads you to understanding the Self. The discovery of the Self through spirituality leads you to personal development and inner growth. In order for that to happen, you must want to know it. When you realize the true Self, which is your true inner being, essence, and makeup, you will attain peace and happiness, which leads to progress and success in your life. All this is hidden in your mind and it is up to you to find it.

Here are some affirmations designed to help you discover your spirituality:

- I am unlimited because the universe is infinite.
- A progressive mind is my true source.
- I will radiate joy and happiness.
- I let my spirit enjoy love and peace.
- I will allow higher power to guide me.
- I choose to let the universe guide me to my highest good.
- Everything happens for a reason.
- I live one day at a time with expectations of good and faith.
- I can handle a higher power in my life.

Visualization

Visualization is extremely important to helping you discover who you are and exploring self-discovery. Visualization is a fantastic tool you can use to help with self-awareness and realization. If you take a moment and just visualize your inner thoughts, it brings you to a heightened level of awareness and to a new dimension. You start to recognize and realize there is so much more to life than just dreaming about doing things. You have the power to do accomplish those dreams. Visualization is a powerful tool used by many successful people, especially business professionals and star athletes.

They use it to help them break through their challenges and to reach the next level. Visualization is used to help with mapping out your goals and beliefs. Visualization helps remove barriers and limitations you may have placed in your own way. Seeing is believing when it comes to visualization but believing will bring about seeing. You can place yourself in any situation when you see yourself doing and successfully accomplishing it. A mental rehearsal will help you achieve great feats by seeing them visually. If you want self-awareness and discovery of the Self, apply these techniques to your life and you will grow into success. Let us rehearse with an exercise. Close your eyes and think about something you need to complete for work.

Imagine the steps you have to take to get the task done, put yourself in that position to start the project and finish the task on time and visualize the results you want. Make it successful. Many great professional athletes and successful actors like Mark McGuire and John Travolta use visualization as a process to achieve phenomenal professional feats beyond the norm; however, this does not speak to their personal life or virtue. Try it and you will see that you are a step closer to awareness.

Focus

Focus is also an important component for self-discovery and understanding the Self. Many people today suffer from lack of focus. Think back on how many times you have started to do something just to end up doing something entirely different. Be honest! How many? Focus is something you can acquire and learn by becoming disciplined and raising your expectations. Focus is a vital part to gaining self-awareness and understanding because without focus, you would be just another helpless, lost soul who is getting by. The sad part is that many of us are that way. Many never take the time to learn who they are, and explore the depth of what their inner being is and the possibility of what could be.

Jimmy, a well-liked stockbroker, used to be an unfocused professional because he just bought whatever hot securities were moving that day. Soon, he discovered that he had accumulated so many securities that he could not possibly keep up with tracking all those stocks and be effective in knowing what was happening with each company. He realized that if he just focused on a handful of companies and learned them all very well, he could make an impact on his clients' financial life. By becoming an expert and focusing on one area, he was able to provide a valuable service that many could use. He distinguished himself from all the other stockbrokers. His practice soared and his income improved tremendously simply by focusing and becoming aware of what he was doing.

Dreams to Goals ... Goals to Reality

Some men see things as they are and say why—I dream things that never were and say why not.
—George Bernard Shaw

When you develop and learn to understand your dreams and goals, you move one step closer to self-awareness and self-realization. Most of the time, your dreams are poorly defined. They are usually vague, general in manner, and not sharply focused. That is why they fail to become a reality. You need to visualize your goals and dreams and see it through in your mind. This brings it a step closer to reality. Ask yourself questions like

- What makes up my dream?
- What is good about it?
- Why is it important?
- What is going on in my life around it?

Think of something tangible you want and attach it to your dreams. This makes it feel real. Picture it in your mind and it will make it very clear to you. When you understand your purpose, you gain awareness. Awareness of what you want from your life is extremely important to finding the self.

To help you gain realizations of your goals, learn to be as specific and descriptive as you can when writing down your goals. Ask yourself questions like

- What exactly?
- Where exactly?

- How long exactly?
- Why exactly
- For whom exactly?

You need to continue to question yourself until you have formalized your dreams into a practical goal. This will provide you with consistent feedback and motivation to move forward with your dreams. When you fulfill your dreams and goals, you are not only closer to fully understanding who you are, you may be able to share the Self with others you care for and love.

Turn Your Goals into Planned Actions

What lies behind us and what lies before us are small matters compared to what lies within us.
—Ralph Waldo Emerson

When your goals are specific, you can determine the amount of time, the financial commitment, and work effort required to achieve it. At this point, you can characterize clearly how much exertion and what type of efforts it will take you to reach the goals that support your dreams. Be realistic, especially if you can control the efforts that will lead to the outcome of your goals. No one plans to win the lottery, but you can plan to make more phone calls and more activities to complete your assigned task at work. Those things will bring you closer to accomplishing your goals. Accomplishing your set goals is one of the steps to the gateway to becoming the person you want to be.

Learn to actualize. What do I need to achieve over time to realize my goal? You should make self-actualizations a permanent part of your routine and life. Ask yourself questions like, "What do I need to do on a daily basis to guarantee I will achieve what I set for myself?" Take action and be consistent!

Chapter Fifteen

Goal Setting

Goal setting is essential to understanding the Self and the discovery of who you are. I mentioned earlier that companies that have a plan tend to succeed more than others do. However, before that can take place, they must set a specific goal. Goals are the foundation for progress. They are the building blocks and the DNA for personal awareness and discovery. Goals need to be specific and detailed in nature. What you need to do is set near-term, short-term, intermediate, and long-term goals.

Near-term goals are things you want to achieve and or accomplish within a twenty-four-hour to a one-month period. When setting these goals, remember that they are usually items you need to achieve to bring something you have been working on to completion. By understanding these near-term goals, it gives you commitment to finishing a set task.

Short-term goals are set with a one-month to six-month timeline in mind. Again, this process allows you to build a foundation of things you need to accomplish to get the results you are looking to achieve.

Intermediate goals are set with a six-month to one-year timeframe. In my opinion, this type of goal setting is essential. I believe it is most important because it provides you with a constant reminder of where you are and what you should be doing. You should constantly be updating, revising, and reviewing these goals. This forces you to become aware because you know where you are now and where you need to be. It allows you to plot out a plan of action, making you focus on the action instead of the results, which will force you to work towards looking at the big picture.

Long-term goals are set with one- to three-year timeframes. Long-term goals along with action steps force your subconscious to work and pay attention. If you know what you want, then it gives you a sense of direction, and when you have direction, you have purpose. When you have purpose, you gain awareness, which in turn leads to understanding the Self. Long-term goals once achieved or attempted will allow you to gain self-discovery and major awareness in your life and that is what you should be striving to achieve.

Chapter Sixteen

Where Are You Now?
Where Do You Want to Go or End Up?

If you're not sure where you are going, you're liable to end up someplace else.
—Robert Mager

Our life is a like a business. What makes a business successful? Some say a great plan and a great product. Others say a great management team, a great idea, a need for the product, and a great marketing campaign. I say it's all of those things assembled together and packaged in a way simple that is easy to explain. A business does not take shape immediately. It has to be nurtured and worked on daily. Its workers and managers must have a plan, a process, and a discipline. Our life is the same way. You must look at the big picture. You must always be looking towards the future. Like any good business, it all starts with a mission statement. You must create a personal mission statement for you. Once you have that in place, you have a starting point. The simpler and more specific your personal mission statement in life is, the more focused you will become. Just like many great businesses that have stayed focused for over one hundred years, and continue to grow exponentially while staying true to their vision and mission statements.

The next thing you must look to create is a vision statement of what you ultimately want and what your life will look like in the future. This is important. A business that has been long lasting and successful possesses a vision statement that it has used to steer and guide it. Do not get confused here; a vision is similar to a mission statement; but very different. Your vision should be an extension of your personal mission statement. Here is an example of a vision statement of a successful weight management company:

> "Alpha Omega is the premier weight loss program and company in the state of Florida. We are true professionals at all times committed to excellence, passionate about making a difference in people's lives and are enthusiastic in delivering our service! We work in highly developed teams, providing life solutions for our patients who we enjoy and who appreciate the unparalleled relationships we offer. Our business grows through well-orchestrated systems of personal desire for development and self-actualization, which we are energetically striving to fulfill. Together we achieve success at levels beyond expectations and therefore become the company of choice for patients and professionals to establish relationships."
> -Dr. Sadhana Shah

Now that is a powerful vision statement. It covers in detail what the company strives to achieve. It states what is important to them, what their objectives are, and how they plan on going about accomplishing it.

Let us look at a personal vision statement. This should give you some ideas to formulate your own personal vision statement. Yours should be as detailed as you want, but make certain it is concise and well thought out. If it is not, you are just wasting your time. Remember, the purpose of your personal vision statement is to be your written visualization exercise of where and how you see yourself in five, ten, fifteen, twenty, and thirty years.

"I am a good, caring, and loving person who is devoted to my family, career, and the well-being of society. It is my intention to educate, learn, and grow my knowledge, my career, and personal fortune by through dedication, focus, and honesty, and being true to the people around me and myself. I want to leave a legacy for my family, children, and society by being committed to my work and community." This person's personal vision statement is very broad, but works for him because he is stating what he sees for himself and the type of person he wants to become.

Each vision statement that you write brings you closer to helping you understand who you are and it will help lead you to where you want to end up in your life. The Self is about understanding that you are about your inner being. I previously mentioned not everyone is brave enough to find out who he or she is and what his or her real essence in life is. Are you ready to find your being? Are you willing to work to find the true Self? If you are, it is up to you to follow and continue to learn and understand it. Let us get back to the original thought where I stated that life is like a business. Remembering this comparison will help you understand where you are and where you need to be. However, only you can decide what you want out of your life. Every business needs to figure out where it stands in its development of products and services that it will provide to its customer. It is no different when it comes to where you are in understanding who you are. You need to figure out what your product or service is in your life. What can you offer to this society and world? The service you have to offer is in your skill, knowledge, and level of education. You need to know what your skill-set is. When you know what your strengths and weaknesses are, you can be honest about them and then you can get closer to understanding the Self. Once you are able to do so, you will be able to understand where you are in your life. This will help you gain some understanding of who you are and where you want to go.

Once you develop your life objectives, it is much easier to see yourself for what you are. In the business world, they call it business strategic objectives and in your personal life, it is called understanding yourself. Once you understand yourself, things will start to take on a new shape. Your sense of awareness is enlightened. Your sense of consciousness and sensitivity is awakened like a nose to the scent of a freshly cut rose. The senses observe it right away.

Compare yourself to a company and understanding that your life is like the working of a business look at your background. What is it that you are most proud of in your life? In business, this lays a foundation for what they do best. By establishing and understanding your background, you can create a level of awareness of your own purpose. All companies and executives have a certain level of knowledge, drive, and expertise they bring to their business to make it successful.

Understand what your background is, and it will be a starting point to figuring out where you stand in your own life and where you want to be or end up. Your personal background gives you a sense of belonging and purpose. This will come in the form of your experiences and the only way you gain experience is by getting involved and participating. By doing things you find interesting, it eventually serves an improved purpose. That is what helps make a business successful. Why not use those same elements to help you gain clarity and understand who you are. Aside from emotional strings in life, what else steers your purpose and background? Once you start to understand that particular issue, you start to gain purpose, which leads you closer to your awareness and helps you understand yourself.

In business, your background and purpose are essential to the creditability and success of that institution and organization. I believe there is no difference with self-discovery. We all have to experience this part of our life to gain acceptance and understanding. The main difference is that in business, you are forced to examine your purpose, vision, mission, and strategic objectives, but in your own life, you never lay out a plan, process, or discipline. Therefore, you are constantly skipping, jumping, and daydreaming about what you want and believe. In business, you cannot afford to do that because time lost can lead to money wasted, opportunity cost and accountability to others who are dependent on your leadership and guidance. However, in your own life, who is holding you up to the measuring stick? Who is holding you accountable? Accountability and measurement is essential to discovering and understanding who and where you are.

As a person gets older and wiser in their life, they assemble and create a sense of history. I know what you are saying, "What does this have to do with self-discovery?" Remember, in all business plans they talk about the business and company history, how it got to where it is today, and how it was able to survive during good times and bad times. The history does not have to be lengthy or extremely detailed, but it must be accurate in its content and it must address a well thought out process.

Like any good business, the Self is on its way to awareness and discovery. It must create a sense of history, events, and experiences. When you are able to go back and write, examine, and formulate all the events you have been through you will be able to create a higher level of awareness. This will bring you closer to self-awareness and understanding the Self. Past successes help prevent mistakes!

Gaining realization and discovery of who you are is not very difficult in this process because your history is your own life. What is difficult is getting to this point. Learn to relive it through pleasurable memories. Your childhood, failures, successes, accomplishments that are in your history are your inner being. It is surely worth gaining an understanding of them and experiencing it because no one else except you can relive that history. In business, the most the company can share with the shareholders are statistics, milestone earnings, new products and innovations, but in self-discovery, you can sit and re-experience your entire history repeatedly. Realization and knowing the Self is forever; gaining greater returns, which cannot ever be lost.

This is how you do it. First, sit in a place where you are most comfortable and at ease. Light a scented candle and make the room temperature just the way you like it. Close your eyes, take three to four deep breaths and let each one out slowly. Start breathing normally and relax. Start to slow your breathing down, feel yourself drifting, and relaxing. Start from the top of your head and relax by letting all the stress go. Imagine yourself in a place so peaceful, so rewarding, and filled with pleasure. Feel the muscles in your face relax. Lick your lips to moisten them as you listen to the blood in your veins flow through your body. Relax your shoulders, and rotate your neck in small circles slowly three times to the left then to the right three times then lean forward and then backwards continuing to breathe slowly. Shake your hands slightly out to your sides keeping your eyes closed. Continue to feel yourself drifting to your special place of peace. Lift your toes off the ground three times, feel the muscles contract and relax while imagining you are sitting on a cloud. Now imagine your best thoughts while counting backwards in your mind from ten. As this starts to happen, place yourself in the memory you want to relive. First, focus on the surroundings, the layout of the situation, the room, and the scent. Begin to discover the history you want to relive and experience. This experience is yours again to enjoy. Live it! Use this technique repeatedly to set the mood and it will help you get relaxed and bring to a state of relaxation. It will put you in a state of awareness as you journey back to your personal history and wonderful memories. Another way to bring you back to your history is to think of your favorite song. If you have one, you will be able to remember where you were when you first heard it and you could bring those memories back quickly without having to try to illicit a response. That is the feeling you want to come away with after you relive your history. You want to gain relaxation, realization, awareness, and understanding. You will experience all that by performing this simple exercise.

Understanding your history makes your life rich and more rewarding. If you perform this exercise from time to time, it will serve as an affirmation to the subconscious and it will help trigger self-discovery and awareness. It will help you understand who you are and will give you the direction you need, but it is up to you to act on it.

Chapter Seventeen

Systems, Processes, and Structure

Professionalism is knowing, how to do it, when to do it, and doing it.
—Frank Tyger

As you review any successful business *plan* and their objectives, you will see that they have a clear and identifiable structure in place, that is a process and system that has been crucial to the success and growth of that business. Structure is an identifiable way one does something in a reoccurring manner. That is why a system and a process are created for the benefit of the business. It brings consistency and predictability to the organization. I find that structure in business is the essential component for its long-term success, progress, and growth. Without this in place from the very beginning, it is doomed. McDonald's is a prime example of a company with excellent processes and systems. McDonald University, which created the process of standardization that, included a system for all locations and restaurants.

This should not be any different for you in your personal life. Think about it for a moment. When has anything you have done extremely well been accomplished on a whim? When you were in grade school or growing up, we had a plan and a structure while attending school. It seems that as we get older and learn to be self-sufficient, we tend to forget the basics of living and understanding. We tend to gravitate to the extreme. You become more lost. To gain better understanding of the Self and learning who you are you will require some sort of structure place. Structure in the personal side of living is even more important as you get older because with age and time comes more responsibility. More expectations are placed on you, which make it even harder for you to function productively without structure in your life.

Sit and think about that for a moment. How many people do you know who are extremely successful, just successful, doing okay, or just getting by? What is the one of the components that truly differentiates the extremely successful individuals from the others you are thinking? Think about how much more successful, positive, outgoing and available that person or persons would be for himself or herself, his or her family, and community if they were organized or had structure in place in their lives? How many of your friends are nice people who are likeable, kind, respectable, and outgoing but they are all over the place. They have so many irons in the fire and never finish what they say they are going to do or start. They never follow through with what they promised to do. What about some of these people who do not have any other extra-curricular activities and yet they cannot find the time to get anything done for himself or herself, his or her family, or community. All that happens are excuses. Is that you or do you know someone like this? Some of these people are very successful financially and personally, but they never have any time to enjoy the fruits of their own labor and when they take a break, they don't know how to really relax and enjoy the time off.

I have a friend who I believe is very structured and successful. His comments to me were, "I wish I could better manage my time so that way I could get more things done in a day." What I found is that he is structured, but he is always looking to improve his situation. He realizes that he could get better in his business and in his personal life by managing his time and his expectations. It is paramount to his overall success.

Let us look at you and determine how to help you gain better understanding, realization, awareness, and self-discovery through structure. Just like any successful business, you must determine what your purpose is and what your wants and desires are. Outline your own life and then create a system and process for dealing with issues and concerns. Structuring the other parts of your life is easy, once you determine what you want to achieve. You need to spend time doing this. Otherwise, you will never gain any insight and realization of yourself, what you want to be, or how you want to be remembered.

Here are some tips for helping you build a better work structure:

- Lay out a process on how you plan to accomplish what you want for this part of your life. If you are a professional, what things do you need to accomplish in order for the expected results to take place? Write them down. For example, if you are a sales consultant and you know that to make one sale you have to make at least five presentations, write down the steps you go through as you prepare for your presentation. Make it a process, and create a system. You will be able to function at a higher level of success because you are systemizing your process. This is just a small example of some of the improvements you can make to help you become more aware.

Chapter Eighteen

———

Family Responsibilities

No man can live happily who regards himself alone, who turns everything to his own advantage. Thou must live for another, if thou wish to live for thyself.
—Seneca

The next concern is family and how this affects your ability to determine where you are and where you want to be. How does family structure help in understanding and determining the Self? Structure is essential in discovering you. When you have a structure, it brings you closer to knowing who you are because it provides you with direction. Some people go through their entire life not knowing their predisposition of themselves or their loved ones. Are you guilty of this? Think. Many people never take the time to learn what is important to them or their loved ones until it is too late. Where do you stand on this? Do you know someone like this? The question is what is important to you, your family, or to your loved ones? Do not wait until it is too late. Are you in this situation?

I had a friend who was so into himself that he never realized his surroundings. He focused on what was best for him and him alone. He never took the time to ask his single mother why she never remarried after his father passed away when he was just three years old, leaving him and his mother alone in a strange country. Doug used to think about his father often, so he would ask his mom questions but he failed to engage in any meaningful conversation with her. Erica was a devoted mother to Doug. He got whatever he wanted and he did whatever he wanted to do. However, Doug was selfish. He never learned to share his feelings, especially those about his deep-rooted issue of feeling empty without a male figure in his life. He never learned how to understand who he is, and he never learned to understand the person closest to him. He neglected to learn why she sacrificed her happiness for him. Doug's grandfather died when his mom was very young and when her mother remarried she never felt accepted by her stepfather. Because of this, Erica never wanted her son to experience those feelings. Erica felt she needed to protect Doug from strangers and outsiders. Because she felt so strong about the issue, she sabotaged her own happiness for Doug's contentment. The sad thing about this issue is that I know what Erica is feeling, but Doug has never taken the time to speak to his mom about her life and feelings. He is always too busy focusing on his needs. He has never understood what is important to his or Erica's life. The structure that was lacking in this situation was open communication between both parties. This is likely to continue until one of them makes the effort to open up to the other and takes action.

When dealing with structure, and how it affects our level of responsibility, you will find it is amazing what you can achieve with a process in place. Successful businesses have detailed systems and processes they follow daily. All assigned tasks performed in a particular way, which makes them easier to accomplish. When you have a system, no matter who is completing a particular task, they will be able to manage it without a struggle because there are specific instructions in place. Structure and discipline is what makes a company great. It differentiates itself from it competition because it has been able to duplicate a system and continuously improve its processes.

For personal growth, you must find, identify, and maintain your own discipline. You have to know what is important to you and build a system and process of structure in your life. It is never too late to start. Structure is very important in understanding who you are. Let us look at a child's life. When a child is born, you set up a feeding schedule and naptime. You have the child take a nap at a specific time. They are put to bed at a certain time. You introduce structure and a routine, to make both your lives easier. Face it, all through your early childhood you experienced structure and some sense of discipline. If you did not get your chores done or finish your homework, you had consequences to face and they were a form of structure for your certain behavior or action. Structure kept you on your toes and in line. It gave you a sense of purpose in your life. Nevertheless, what happens as you get older and you do not have to answer to anyone? When you remove structure from your life that is when you stop personal growth. You lose a sense of who you are. Just like anything else, the longer you ignore something, the tougher it is going to be to regain control of it.

I can give you hundreds of examples of people who lacked discipline in their life and never understood who they really are. A prime example is boxer Mike Tyson. He does not know who he really is or what he stands for. He does not understand the Self. If he did, he would not continue to make the same mistakes repeatedly. I am a huge boxing fan and to see a person of Mike Tyson's great talent end up in the state that he is in, saddens me greatly. In Mike Tyson's case, he had no real structure in his life. At one point, he was a juvenile delinquent, but once he found and discovered structure he was able to channel his energy and mind towards a positive source. He was able to become one of the greatest heavy weight boxers in the last fifty years. However, when Tyson lost that structure in his life it went downhill. When his trainer and adopted father passed away, his life fell apart, and has been on a downward spiral ever since. He lost the only structure he really had. No matter what he might have done, in Cus D'Amato's eyes he would still have been the same Mike Tyson. He would have been the same person and would have been treated the same way. He would have to follow the rules.

When Mike became the champion, he was in charge. He was a lager-than-life character, but he wasn't prepared for a life of fame. What Mike rebelled against for so many years was not a consideration any more and it led him down the path of destruction because he did not have to answer to anyone. It was a chaotic situation and you can witness the results.

Another example of a person who lacked structure in his life leading him down the path of self-obliteration is Jack Osborne, Ozzy Osborne's son from the TV program *The Osborne's*. Jack is a classic person who has no respect for structure. He was left alone to make mistakes and it sent him to rehab. Jack started to abuse drugs and alcohol and it forced him to be placed in a drug treatment center because of his lack of self-respect and self-worth. Jack does not know the Self. He is the result of no direction and discipline.

Now let us look at what a well thought out and structured person's life can bring. Arnold Schwarzenegger is a man who has structure and self-discipline in his life. This world-class body builder, box-office superstar, politician, and most recently Governor to the state of California has achieved great accomplishments by viewing success as a process. Who would have thought a once skinny Austrian with a heavy accent from Eastern Europe would amass a personal fortune of over $200 million and remain as grounded as he has? Arnold Schwarzenegger truly understands the Self. He knows what is important to him. He shows it everywhere he goes. Arnold has had structure in his life from the very beginning, which molded him into what he is today. From an early age, his father was a disciplinarian, who felt he had to do all his homework and chores before he could go outside, play, and hang out. From a very early beginning, he learned that he had to do the basics to get ahead and follow a plan and process to succeed in life.

He figured out that in order for him to get better at something, he had to have a plan and be committed. At that early age, he learned he had to be disciplined, and follow a structure and have a process in his daily life and most importantly stick with it. He wanted to be famous like the bodybuilders he read about in the magazines. He wanted to be rich and travel the world. The way he decided to achieve these goals was through bodybuilding. What was instinctual to Arnold was that he wrote down his life goals on paper. He took the time and worked towards creating a process and structure for what he wanted to achieve in his life. He learned what we all are seeking. He discovered at a very early age in his life the Self that made him tick. He discovered what his essence and being is. If he did not know then when he took the time to write down his goals and desires, he surely knows it now. Arnold wrote out what exactly what he wanted. From where sit he has accomplished exactly what he set out to do and more and when he first realized what he wanted for his life. He proceeded without hesitation. Arnold is a prime example of what structure and discipline can do for a person who follows a plan, process, and discipline. I know I did not give you all the details on how Arnold got where he is today. It is up to you to figure out who you are, where you need to be, and what you want out of your own life. The self is right there for you to discover, it's all yours for the taking. Gandhi, said, "We must be the change we wish to see." Mary Kay Ash once said, "Those who are blessed with the most talent don't necessarily outperform everyone else. It's the people with follow through who excel." How do you want to be remembered? What steps are you going to take? Are you willing to sacrifice the time and make the commitment to what you want in your life?

Chapter Nineteen

Reflections

All mankind is divided into three classes: those that are immoveable, those that are movable and those that move.
—Ben Franklin

When you address all the thoughts you have in your mind, it is sometimes difficult to gather your faculty together. The only way I believe you are truly able to do so or understand all that is happening at any given time, is to learn how to reflect on your situation. The Self is like fine wine. It needs to sit for a while to observe its surroundings. You cannot rush change; you have to reflect on what is happening around you. Play it out in your mind after the event or situation has taken place, then you can truly evaluate effectively. Perhaps the situation did not turn out the way you planned, but this is the right time. Regardless, look at what went right or wrong and learn from it. Do not dwell on what happened, use the event to learn from and use as experience and discovery, and understand the Self. Accept it, free it, and nurture it. Once you are able to get this point in your life you are on your way to knowing the "Self," fulfillment and personal growth and development is just right around the corner. Can you feel it?

My friend Chris is a successful mortgage broker, he works very hard, and he expects the best at all times. A large company refinanced a deal that Chris was working on for over six months and through no fault of his own, he lost the deal to a competing company. He wanted to know why he lost the contract because he had placed so much time, effort, and expectation on this project. He wanted to know how he could have done to win the deal. The fact was, he could have controlled the mishap, but he did not. He came to me for help and I asked him to reflect on what happened during the deal to use it as a learning experience for the future and repeat the mistake.

Chris took my advice and learned from this experience. He figured out if he was paying attention to the client's likes and dislikes, he would have won the contract because he did not lose the loan because of rates, he lost it because the other broker developed a relationship with the client and made them feel he had their best interest at heart. He failed to engage with the prospects.

Chris took this loss and turned it into a positive experience and this has helped him win several contracts that were bigger than what was lost. His ability to reflect on this situation and monetary loss allowed him to become more aware of his surroundings and at the same time made him a better professional.

Chapter Twenty

Hierarchy of Life

What you value is what you think about. What you think about is what you become.
—Joel Weldon

The way you see yourself is the way your life will be! Self-fulfilling prophecy will be determined by the way you live your life. In understanding the Self you must first learn about the hierarchy of life. Knowing where you are and what is important to you will take you a long way in self-discovery and becoming more aware. I believe it is imperative that you know and understand the workings of the hierarchy of life. The hierarchy of life is not a new concept. Maslowe talked about this many years ago, but I believe you have to concentrate in knowing and understanding the following:

- You
- Family
- Community
- Purpose
- Structure

The hierarchy of living, first phase is learning about you, the individual. We all need to know who we are. Once you know what you are all about and what you stand for and represent then you should be able to focus on all the important things in your own life. Here are some questions you must ask yourself in order to discover you:

- What is important in my life?
- Am I living up to my potential?
- What is my legacy going to be like?
- Am I comfortable with my life?
- Have I accomplished what I want to achieve thus far?

You see in order for you to know the "Self," you must know what you want out of your life and then you can become aware and discover the Self. Until you do so, you will be running on the treadmill of life, moving, but going no particular place.

Phase two in the hierarchy of living is family. You must know how important your family is to you. Many of us never learn to accept and understand the importance of family. We tend to take it for granted. The family bond and support system is essential to the Self and its discovery. Family is significant because it helps develop and identify what the self is going to be like. Most people do not put family first; usually it's last on their list of priorities. In the hierarchy of living, people who have close and interactive ties with their family are comfortable with them already and tend to be more happy and productive because they have a support group and encouragement along the way of their progress and personal growth. Reflect on this for a moment and think about where you are at this moment within your family!

You cannot do for your family first unless you do for you first. The people who can understand this concept will discover the Self and learn awareness quicker than those who do not. Family is an important and a significant part of the self because it offers and provides a foundation to what is or could be important to you in life.

The third phase of the hierarchy of living is community. In order for you to be a credit to your community, you must know "you" then understand and support your family. Then you can give back to your community. Community is important and crucial to self-development. You can know the Self and become aware while giving back to the place where you live and help shape the Self. Community offers you a place for you to leave your mark or legacy. You cannot become a part of your community overnight, but you can participate and then gradually gain awareness and acceptance. When you participate, you can discover the Self because you are creating opportunities to learn, discover, and explore what else is out there and how it will or could impact you. Community is essential to the Self and your own awareness. It is up to you to participate and seek its guidance. Community participation does not have to consume your life, but the involvement must make a difference to you and the people involved. Voting is not community participation or involvement. You must actually find and commit to making a difference to other people. Volunteer at a soup kitchen, work with disadvantage children, and find something that will give your life purpose. This is a way of unleashing the self-factor in us.

The fourth phase of the hierarchy of living is purpose. What is your purpose life? Do you know? Do you even care? If you can answer these questions then you are a lot closer than many to knowing the Self. When you have a real sense of purpose, you then become aware of your existence. When you can share what is important to you with others freely and aren't wrapped up with your ego or being selfish then you can gain awareness and surely start to know the Self. This is when you are confirming your life's purpose. Purpose is a way of feeling needed and wanted.

The fifth and final element to the hierarchy of living is structure. I touched on structure in detail in earlier chapters, but structure is important enough that you need to know why it fits into the hierarchy of life. Structure is your guide rail. It allows you to make improvements in your life without going off the deep end. With structure, you are able to be disciplined and see things through to the finish. Structure reminds you to be real and not take anything for granted because once you are focused on getting things completed; you are closer to understanding the Self and gaining awareness in your life.

13 points to help discover the Self
By Dr. Ram P. Ramcharran

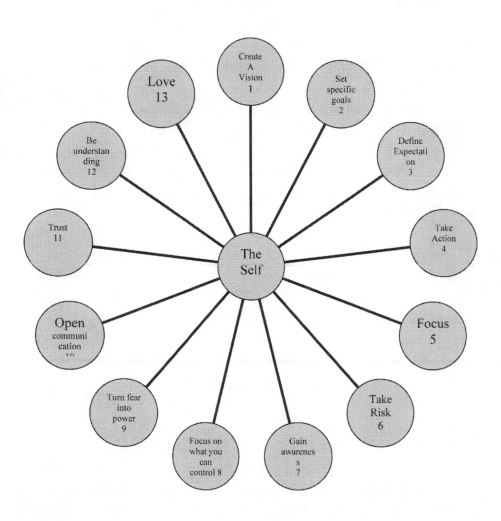

Chapter Twenty-One

Steps to Help You Discover and
Understand the Self.

In order for you to know the "Self," I believe there are a number of things you need to learn which will specifically lead to you discovering the Self. Once you discover the Self, then you can go on to understanding and then improving the Self.

Create a Vision
A clear vision is the driving force behind the Self and your overall make up as a person. A clear vision helps you establish commitment and focus towards personal growth. Vision is the DNA and building block of the Self. Once you are able to follow your vision effectively, you are on your way to finding and understanding the Self.

Set Specific Goals
Goals help take you to the next level in life. You must learn to move out of your comfort zone. Goals give you direction and help remove restrictions and limitations by helping you achieve your task. Establishing specific goals and laying out your action steps provides a plan, a process, and a discipline. Once those items are in place, you have the tools to succeed. You are on your way.

Define Expectations

Expectations create authority and gives you a level of outcome of what to expect. The outcome you are looking for helps you understand. It provides boundaries, authority, support, and resources of what is needed to occur in order to get the correct outcome. This is an important part of gaining awareness.

Take Action

Do not wait for things to happen. You need to set the pace and lead from the front. Create your own destiny because you can control the activities and actions taken. No one else but you can do this! Set the example and expect the results you are seeking.

Focus

Allows you to become committed to what you are doing. Focus brings commitment making you an integral part of the creation of the outcome of the event or situation. Focus brings you closer to your beliefs and the results you are seeking to achieve. This puts you in charge. You are leading from the front, not playing catch up!

Take Risks

Risk is the catalyst for growth, learning, change, and innovations. Encouraging calculated risk taking will help self-discovery. Without risk, you are destined to be sedentary in your life and tend to settle for less. The benefits of risk for the most part outweigh the results of playing it safe.

Gain Awareness

Paying attention allows you to see things more clearly that you might have otherwise missed. Awareness improves communication and enhances the self and the people around you. It is extremely important to improving the Self. When you have awareness, you are able to communicate more clearly and effectively.

Focus on What You Can Control

Do not dwell on failures or past successes. Do not live your life looking in the rear view mirror. "Why worry?" When you move forward and continually look ahead in life, you are learning and discovering life around you. Do not place limitations on your life! When you do so, you limit your success and self-development. Sometimes you have to deal with the problem directly and lead.

Turn Fear into Power by Taking Action

Fear is false evidence appearing real. How you allow fears to affect you will determine your growth and progress in life. You need to understand that all fears can be overcome and conquered. Fears can be turned into action just by identifying and understanding it. Once you do this, you are that much closer to Self-discovery.

Open Communication

What you say and how you say it is how others decide to perceive you. When you take personal responsibility for your communication and actions, then you display integrity. This defines your role when you are able to communicate effectively. You become like a magnet when you can communicate effectively and openly.

Trust

Trust comes from faith. Self-trust and trusting others gives you the ability to create change and improve your life. This is essential to self-discovery. Without trust in your life, you are not going to experience true personal growth. You need trust in your life because it is essential to Self-discovery and your awareness. Look at the people, who lack faith, they also have very little trust in others. Do not confuse trust with being cautious in your life decisions.

Be Understanding

Since change is rapid, you need not be so rigid. Flexibility allows for a faster course of action, less stress and quicker response to problems. By allowing yourself to be flexible, it gives you the upper hand when problems or the unexpected occur. Being calm, collected, and sensible will provide you the advantage of thinking clearly. Reverse the situation for a moment and then take action, it allows for a better response.

Love

"Love is letting go of fear" according to Dr. Gerald Jampolsky. True love is unconditional. Love is the most empowering filter you can look through, because when you choose to see the world through the eyes of love, you respect the dignity of others and reduce negative stress in yourself and others. Love is true friendship and true friends give without expecting anything in return. Impure love is selfish- always wanting something in return. Is your love that way?

Chapter Twenty-Two

Steps to Help You Make Improvement to the Self

You are what your deep, driving desire is. As your
desire is, so is your will. As your will is, so your
deed. is your deed is, so is your destiny.
—Brihad, IV

Step one

Align your expectations. When you set expectations and they are met, you become extremely happy; while on the other hand, when expectations are set and are not met, you become extremely annoyed and angry. Self-talk is extremely important for your emotional wellness. Setting the correct expectations and receiving the chosen results will bring greatest satisfaction.

Step two

Keep a continuous process. You have to keep the focus on moving forward in your life. If you cannot do so, you are setting yourself up for a letdown. When you make a decision and follow through, it provides continuity and commitment. It demonstrates that you are taking the necessary steps to enable the results. Always look to make improvements in your life.

Step three

Trust. As simple as this may seem, it is extremely important to achieving successful changes in your behavior and attitude. You have to trust you are making the right decision. Without real trust, you will be spinning your wheels. You have to believe and trust that you are making the right decisions. Do not second-guess your decisions. Trust will bring you new discovery in your life.

Step four

Form a new picture. Take a new picture. Redefine yourself, your goals, and your objectives. Do not forget about the old—keep them as a reference point, use them for reflection and use them to close the gap between where you are and where you want to be. The new picture provides inspiration and motivation. It is like a new environment and change. If you apply and visualize it, you are closer to gaining the awareness and understanding that you are seeking.

Step five

Always help others. Be a listener and share your experiences. By applying the golden rule to each situation and life, it makes you more aware of what is happening around you and at the same time, gives you strength to move ahead and create changes and make improvements. Helping others will help you feel good inside. When you are experiencing warm and fuzzy feelings from helping others, you are learning about the Self. You cannot manufacturer these feelings artificially. Do not be afraid to help others, especially if you do not expect anything back in return. You will gain awareness! Trust me!

Step six

Be thankful. This is what you can have full control over, because no one else can do this for you. It is up to only you to say thank you and for it to be meaningful. When you are thankful, you are not taking anything for granted in your life. Many go through life expecting the world to give them something or acting as if they are owed something. Let that not be you! Self-discovery, gaining awareness and understanding; all these elements come from being thankful. When you say, "Thank you" and truly mean it, then you are truly closer to knowing the Self.

Epilogue

It is time to change and it is up to you to make the improvement. This book is not simply a prescription for success in learning how to understand the Self and discover who you are. It is a manual on how to go about doing so.

How you feel, think, and act is a direct result of how you know yourself and what level you are willing to reach. Boundaries that once restricted you can now be challenged and faced directly. The rules of life are constantly changing and without a process, a plan, discipline, and structure, it makes it difficult for you to improve and discover the Self.

This book is really about bridging the gap between where you are and learning to discover where you want and need to be to discover the Self. Learning about your inner being can take you to new heights in your life and it is up to you and you alone to do so. The Self is a place where you have absolute control. Take action now!

Become responsive and learn to be real and discover the real you. Those of you who engage in this process of discovery must remember your self-development is unlimited and it is your responsibility to share it with your loved ones. The Self becomes a symbol for life and you must live it, enjoy it, make it active, and *discover* it.

Get started today!
Dr. Ram

About the Author

Dr. Ram P. Ramcharran is a behavioral counselor. He is passionate about helping others with their self-development, discovering self- awareness, self-trust, and personal acceptance.

Ram has developed programs on behavioral finance, weight management, and working effectively in large groups. He has helped teams and organizations to understand their clients and customers. He has written several articles on self-esteem, awareness, performance anxiety, productivity, and weight management.

Dr. Ramcharran is a popular speaker among many local groups, national organizations, and companies. He has been a guest on several local talk-radio programs speaking about weight management and peak performance. He has developed and administered workshops and classes on leadership, making life changes, weight loss management, stress management, motivation, and understanding and discovering the Self.

Dr. Ram and his family reside in Tarpon Springs, Florida.